# UN-MASKED
# UN-BROKEN
## HEALED & SET FREE

*A Journey of Healing, Liberation,*
*and Redemption*

# TAMI FRANKLIN

Un-Masked, Un-Broken, Healed & Set Free

A Journey of Healing, Liberation, and Redemption

Un-Masked, Un-Broken, Healed & Set Free, LLC

ISBN: 979-8-218-26913-5

Book Design by Transcendent Publishing
Editing by Mary Rembert
Book Cover Photography by Heather J. Kirk / Abundant Eight Creative

Printed in the United States of America.

# CONTENTS

# AUTHOR'S NOTE

This memoir is a reflection of my lived experience—my truth, as I walked through it, survived it, and, by the grace of God, began to heal from it. The memories shared here are based on what I remember, what I felt, and what shaped me. While I've done my best to accurately recount events, some names, locations, and identifying details have been changed to protect the privacy of those involved.

Throughout these pages, I speak honestly about deeply personal and painful events. At times, this includes matters of a legal or criminal nature. Please know: I am not here to accuse, defend, or litigate. I share only what I carried, what I witnessed, and what I lived.

There was a time when I attempted to share what I knew with law enforcement, including arranging to speak with a local sergeant. That meeting never took place. What followed was a season of confusion, fear, and trauma that no one is ever truly prepared for. I did what I could at the time with the knowledge, safety, and emotional capacity I had.

Abuse doesn't just wound the body; it distorts trust, reshapes reasoning, and can silence even the strongest voice. I often found myself justifying the unjustifiable, not out of ignorance but out of survival. If you've been there, I see you. This book was written with you in mind.

This story is not about blame; it is about freedom. It is not about perfection—it is about redemption. My prayer is that, in sharing this truth, others will find healing in theirs.

*"You intended to harm me, but God intended it for good to accomplish what is now being done, the saving of many lives."*

— Genesis 50:20

With love,
Tami Franklin
Author of *Un-Masked, Un-Broken, Healed & Set Free*

# MEETING WITH GOD

*"Call to me and I will answer you and tell you great
and unsearchable things you do not know."*

–Jeremiah 33:3, NIV

As I'm writing this, it has been about 30 days since my sweetheart Brittani passed away. Brittani, or Brit as I called her, was the oldest of my five kids. She was 22 years old and passed away after a five-and-a-half-year battle with a rare form of cancer called chordoma.

The cancer was discovered in 2006 after Brit kept complaining about extreme back pain. After taking her to our family doctor for over a year and a half and receiving different explanations of what it could be, the doctor FINALLY suggested we do an X-ray of her chest to see what it would reveal. Before we made it home from having the X-ray, a call came in on my cell phone from the doctor's nurse.

When I answered, the panicked nurse on the other end blurted, "You need to take Brittani to the nearest emergency room *as soon as possible*! She has a 16-inch tumor on her spine!

*Why* did you wait over a week to take her for the X-ray anyway?!"

All I could think was, *How can I possibly begin to answer such a question when I had just received life-changing news about my daughter?!*

To this day, I have no idea how that call ended, but I know it didn't end well, and all I could do was get Brit to the nearest emergency room while dodging through rush hour. The question of delay hung heavily, but words were rendered meaningless in the face of such life-threatening, earth-shattering news.

Fast forward to 2012, and my life has taken multiple unforeseen turns. I find myself in a physical battle against a puzzling, bizarre, and rare ailment—bronchiolitis obliterans organizing pneumonia (BOOP), which I have been battling since September 2011.

As the illness tightens its grip, I am bedridden, immobilized by physical and emotional turmoil. Bereavement and my health struggles force me to confront an uncomfortable truth: I am compelled to confront my existence head-on. Coincidentally, on the very day I was diagnosed with pneumonia, we received the news that Brit's dad, Sherman, had passed away from pneumonia.

At 40 years old, I'm a wife, mom to five, and a dedicated full-time employee, pouring myself into a demanding job that has been a great distraction to keep me from facing myself and my life, but now I'm on a leave of absence for grief.

I am severely depressed and in a deep, dark place—one that I've never been in before. I've suffered from bouts of depression in my teens and early 20s, but nothing EVER like this experience. Afraid and confused, I just don't have the strength or desire to live anymore. I'm not suicidal, but as I lie in this bed day after day, waiting for my husband and children to serve me, I'm sinking deeper and deeper into this pit of the unknown.

One morning, my daughter, Briana (we call her Bri for short), walked into the room to check on me and found me crying uncontrollably.

She said, "What's wrong, Mom?!"

And I told her, "I don't want to live anymore. I don't want to live like this. My life is nothing, and I just don't want to live."

With a complete look of shock, she yelled, "WHAT?! How can you say that?! MOM, WE NEED YOU! The people you inspire need you. You have so much to live for. You've always told us there's nothing in this world that's worth your life. How can you say that now?!"

As my tears flowed uncontrollably, I said, "I live in this bed. I can't walk; I can't work; I can't take care of you, your brother, your sister, or your dad. What use do I have here anymore?"

Bri wouldn't hear any of it. She stood firm on speaking words of encouragement and life back into me. It was almost as if Grammy's spirit was speaking to me through her.

Once I was calm again, she hugged me, said she loved me, and left the room. I lay in that bed, knowing in my heart this strong feeling of not wanting to live was still tugging at me. It just wouldn't rest, no matter what I did.

I had experienced my worst nightmare—burying my child. I am numb; I am so lost; my soul is raw, bruised, damaged beyond repair. It feels as if my life is indescribably broken. There are no words to describe the level of emotional pain I'm feeling. At this point, I can't even see the good in watching my other kids grow older and become adults.

I even imagine that I might not ever heal. I'm at a whole new level of rock bottom, and this time, I can't muster up the courage or strength to begin to pick myself up.

As I lay there, I began to weep, and once the tears began to fall again, the floodgates opened up like the levees were broken, and there were no longer any barriers preventing them from flooding the nearby towns.

Since Brit passed, I've cried oceans of tears, and usually, when I start crying, I can easily cry for five or six hours. Sometimes, it lasts longer. I'm so DEEPLY grieved!

By hour six, I was exhausted from crying, and it didn't look like there was an end in sight. This pain is beyond horrible and indescribable, and I have so many more tears to cry before I reach the bottom of this round. My eyes are swollen, and my nose is so stuffed I can only breathe through my mouth, yet another wave of tears and wailing begins, and I can't stop it this time.

I sat up in my bed and turned my feet to the side in an attempt to get out of bed. My lower extremities, weak from being ill and from all the medications I was taking, left me with no strength to stand on my own. I fell to the ground and crawled to the end of my bed until I couldn't move anymore.

On the ground, I cried and wailed, cried and wailed, cried and wailed until I began to call out, "GOD, I NEED YOU TO HELP ME!" I repeated it over and over again. "GOD, I NEED YOU TO HELP ME! GOD, I NEED YOU TO HELP ME!"

All of a sudden, I heard an audible voice say to me, "My child, I allowed this affliction to come upon you to slow you down long enough to take a good, long look at your life. You've filled your days with caring for everyone else BUT you! You've poured yourself into work, so much so that you've missed out on so much life with your kids: their basketball and football games, as well as graduations.

"Now, tell me if THIS is the life you want for yourself. Because if it is, so shall it be. BUT if it isn't the life you want, I have a much better life planned for you. A life of complete healing, happiness, and abundant blessings for you and your children. Is that the life you want?"

I screamed, "YES, LORD! Yes, yes, yes, that's the life I want for me and my children because I know I won't survive living like this much longer."

He replied, "Before you give me a 'yes,' I want to caution you that your yes will mean that you will have to leave your kids behind at some point to follow the path I have planned for you. Do I still have your yes?"

Without even a single moment of hesitation, I said, "YES, FATHER! You have my complete YES!"

At that very moment, on the floor, in the middle of my bedroom, I gave my yes to the Lord. I took a deep breath, which felt much like the first breath I'd ever taken in my entire life!

It is there that my life and this story really began.

CHAPTER 1

# WHAT REALLY MATTERS

*"There is no greater agony than bearing
an untold story inside you."*

—Maya Angelou

I must say, this is an emotional process. Revealing what has lived *safely* in the darkness of my soul is hard. I can cry down there. I can be frustrated, and I can miss my little girl without ever having to let the world into that sacred space.

But I'm older now. With time, I have come to a different level of courage and desire to say what needs to be said so others can hear what needs to be heard. My story may not be yours, but as my mother-in-law used to say, "We all live in the same house; we just have different addresses." People often talk about why the caged bird sings. My question is, what is the song? This is my address. This is my song.

I was only five years old when my mom went into the hospital for a rather basic procedure, tubal ligation, which is the medical way of saying she was getting her tubes tied. During the operation, the doctor found that her fallopian tubes were wrapped around her bowel tract. When he tried to perform a procedure to separate the two organs, he negligently ripped her bowels.

Mom went into the hospital as an otherwise healthy young woman in her 20s. She left with a colostomy bag and the dire prediction that her days on earth were numbered.

In church on Sundays, I recall the Church Mothers would talk about my mother's pending death right in front of me as if I weren't even there. There was no time for emotions, however. My family jumped right into action, but as a child, I still had unanswered questions.

What did death even mean? Did this mean Mom was leaving me? Will I be allowed to visit on certain days? Couldn't Mom just go back to the hospital and get her body fixed? Would I have to live with that guy they said was my dad? And why can't Grammy make things better?

I didn't know what to do. There were no trained trauma counselors around to help a terrified little girl deal with this kind of confusion and trauma. People were talking all around me, BUT NOBODY WAS TALKING TO ME!

Mom spent several months hospitalized while I stayed with my grandparents. She was eventually discharged and came home. Grammy was the caregiver now, and I watched her love in action every day. I learned a few things myself. At five years of age, I learned how to change a colostomy bag. *If I can only do everything just right,* I remember thinking, maybe she'll get better and stay with us forever. So I stayed focused, tending to my mom and helping my Grammy help her.

Mom slowly recovered enough to attend church with us on Sundays. When she was well enough, she took my brother and me on our traditional after-church drives to look at the big, beautiful homes like the ones Grammy cleaned.

Mom would drive slowly through these manicured neighborhoods, while my brother Tim and I would "oooh and aah" at houses that seemed like a dream that could never happen for us. We would point to houses and notice luxuries like swimming pools and tennis courts. This always hit my spirit very deeply, and I was in awe of how other people lived. I knew I wanted a house like one of those someday, but I didn't want Grammy to clean it. I wanted her to live there too.

Our Sunday drives would be cut short, though, when we'd have to leave those neighborhoods to find a place to change Mom's colostomy bag. She eventually had another surgery to repair the bowel and remove the bag. My Mom recovered fully, thank God!

Eventually, she went back to work again, pulled down enough money to support my brother and me, and we semi-resumed our former routine. Due to a lack of finances, we (my mom, brother, and I) moved habitually from place to place, relocating at least once a year, it seemed, sometimes more.

As a result, my family experienced extended periods of instability. Many people close to me then were unaware of this reality. The term for our circumstances, "homelessness," remained unspoken and unused.

We slept on couches at different friends' houses and crashed with family members. I'd stay with Grammy and Grandpa during the day, often taking a bus there in the early morning with Mom. She'd drop me off and return many hours later, leaving me there while she worked two jobs, sometimes three. It seemed Mom worked constantly, always trying to earn a little extra to make ends meet, but never quite able to pull it off. There was still never enough money for rent or new clothes, and sometimes, there was not even enough for food.

As a child, I didn't realize we were homeless. Looking back, I realize it taught me valuable principles I would have *never* learned if I had a stable home environment. Sharing these moments with my family provided a wealth of experiences that helped me become who I am today.

Most people avoid these truths: Our weaknesses are far more valuable than our strengths. Our failures are far more valuable than our successes. This is one of the reasons why some people exhibit remarkable strength and unwavering resilience! Circumstances leave no alternative.

A praying grandmother is one of the cornerstones that has held families together, much like mine. I'd go so far as to say it is almost mandatory if you are to survive. Grandmothers come with the territory. They help cushion the ride. I had two of the best grandmothers in the world! Their names were Alice Jackson, aka Grammy, and Estell Franklin, aka Grandma Estell.

I was raised mostly with my Grammy. Grammy, who worked cleaning houses for others, was very wise, very strong, and very loving. Sometimes, we didn't have enough food, but Grammy always did. Sometimes, we couldn't pay all the bills, but Grammy always found a way to help. Her home was my special haven, a place of safety, comfort, and the best home cooking on earth. Her love was my foundation, and her hugs seemed to say, "Everything is gonna be alright." She was my best friend, my confidante, and, in at least one literal instance, my savior.

I remember one time when I pulled the classic dumb kid move and swallowed a half dozen metal coins. Why? I don't know. Maybe they looked tasty. Maybe I'd seen Underdog bite one in the cartoons. Regardless of the motivation, the coins lodged in my throat, and I couldn't breathe.

I gasped for breath, turning colors and starting to lose consciousness. Mom looked at me and screamed. She tried to help, and then she called Grammy on the phone. Even though she was eleven blocks away, Grammy got there in minutes, probably driving madly through the streets of Maywood, Illinois, laser-focused.

She burst into the house, and before I knew it, her fingers were down my throat. She grabbed me, and I gagged until the coins came out and were tossed across the kitchen floor. She went in again, making sure no change was left. Thankfully, I was OK. She gave me bread to eat to push anything left in my throat down to my stomach.

Since I was okay, it was time for punishment. Those familiar with this pattern understand it all too well. Once we are over the catalyst event, we are asked, "What were you thinking?!" Grammy was relieved and upset at the same time. There was enough change on the kitchen floor to buy a pack of gum and enough anger in Grammy's voice for me never to swallow coins again.

Even though it's been years since Grammy passed, I can still feel how it felt to be held in her arms. She offered unconditional love. Whether it was whooping my butt when I needed it, making the greatest dinner, or just spending time with me, she was love, and I didn't know it at the time, but I would need it for the days that were headed my way.

My grandmothers were not the only anchors in my life. We were also deeply rooted in the church. My grandfather, in fact, was very important in the church. Although he was not the pastor, he did several things to help our church community. To this day, I still believe he had a calling on his life to be a minister. In fact, he could have been the pastor; all he needed was the title. Grandpa had keys to the church building, and it wasn't uncommon for us to be at church three or four times a week, going early and staying late.

My grandparents and my mom taught us about Jesus, placing a strong belief system within me and a solid foundation of faith that endures to this very day. In a life outsiders might view as chaotic and untethered, the church gave me a feeling of stability. There was love inside those walls. From my grandparents to the preacher to those ever-present women we called Church Mothers, who cared for kids like me with the option of whooping our butts if the situation merited, we knew we were loved. And the rule was, if you got whooped at church or even in the neighborhood, you'd get it *again* at home. I remember those church days. They were the best times of my young life, and only got better once I met my father.

*"Dad!" I yelled at the top of my imaginary voice.*

*"Tami!" My dad called back. He embraced me warmly and tightly and asked me to sit down.*

*"I've got our favorite drink," he said.*

*"Black coffee! Yay!" I was so excited as I plopped down beside him.*

*Dad always drank black coffee with no cream and sugar, and that's why I do, too. He poured me a steaming cup, and we clinked coffee mugs simultaneously and laughed. There were no words, only the energy of mental telepathy between us.*

*We sat there, side-by-side, Dad and I, drinking our black coffee, saying not a word, and having the most enjoyable of conversations. Dad would think something, and his thoughts would pop right into my head. Then I'd reply and put my message right into his consciousness. It was a peaceful and sacred time. We said everything that needed to be said without actually saying a word.*

*All morning long, Dad and I sat on a back porch somewhere, drinking coffee and chatting away silently. It was quiet and as peaceful and restful as I imagine it to be in Heaven.*

*"Everything's going to be alright," Dad thought.*

*I heard him. I believed him. And I received his quiet assurance.*

A year earlier, when I was about four and a half years old, I met my dad for the first time in real life, not in a dream. When we first met, we were living in the same house where I had swallowed those coins. I was at home. It was a normal day—nothing out of the ordinary, just the three of us. Then Mom yelled out, "Tami, get ready. Your dad is coming to pick you up. He's right around the corner."

My mom said it so matter-of-factly as if she were telling me to hurry up or we'd miss the bus or something, which was part of my normal day-to-day life for us then. It took a minute to register those three sentences. At first, I thought I'd misheard. I hadn't.

"My dad?!" I asked.

"Yes, Tami, your *dad*. He'll be here any minute, and he wants to see you."

I panicked! My stomach filled with butterflies. I had no father. At least, none I knew of. I'd heard his name mentioned, of course. I'd certainly never laid eyes on him that I could recall. To me, there was some guy named Richmond out there who was supposedly my dad, but as a young girl, I hadn't given his existence much thought beyond that.

"Tami, hurry *up*. Your dad's on his way. He'll be here any minute."

I froze! Then I ran through the house, terrified. I was not leaving my home with some strange man, even if they did say he was my father. *What's a Dad anyway?* I thought. I had no dad. The only man I'd ever been around consistently was Grandpa. *This guy, whoever he was, could hang out with somebody else today,* I thought. Anybody else but me.

I was in my hiding place, a good one, when I heard "my dad" enter my home. I heard his voice for the first time, making small talk with Mom. It was amazing and disturbing at the same time.

"Tami will be right out," my mother said incorrectly. There was no way I'd be right out, not with this hiding place, not as long as that guy was out there looking for me.

"Tami, come on out," Mom said again. But I wasn't moving. A few seconds after I hadn't appeared, I could hear my mother's footsteps as she began walking through the rooms of our home, looking for me.

"Tami, come out right now!" Mom said again, this time her voice rising. "Your father is here."

It took her a while to find my hiding spot, but she did. I sat there curled up, frozen with fear, scared of who this man was and what it might mean to my young life.

"Mom, please. No. I don't want to go," I pleaded with her.

"Get up. He's ready to see you!"

I relented.

Shaking nervously, I left my hiding place. Mom took me by the hand and led me toward our living room. It was the longest few steps of my life. When we walked into the room, Mom dropped my hand, turned around, and left without a word. There were no introductions, no niceties exchanged, nothing. She dropped me off with my dad. I guess she knew I would eventually be OK.

There was silence. We looked at each other.

"Hi, Tami," said this guy who supposedly was my dad.

"Hi," I said, looking at the floor.

"Let's go," he said. And we did.

It is important to understand how different this was for me. We had no man in our home. The only male who had any influence or say-so was my older brother, Tim, who was actually a young kid too at the time. Mom often appointed him as head of the household when she wasn't around. He cherished that role, often basking in it.

As siblings, we had an oil-and-water relationship during our younger years. Tim took being in charge a little too seriously for me, and I was defiant about it. In my young mind, I was not going to be disciplined by my brother. No way! I resented the thought of some nine-year-old boy telling me what to do. It was crazy. *What did he know that I didn't know anyway?* I thought.

But then Jeannine arrived, and a significant change occurred. It's worth noting that Mom had previously discussed with Tim and me the possibility of becoming a foster mother. Nevertheless, given our preparedness, her decision to proceed was met with a sense of eagerness. It seemed as if one day, it was just Tim and me in our home, playing and fighting as brothers and sisters do. Then, almost overnight, our household gained an older sister, and the order of everything suddenly shifted.

From the day she came into our home, Jeannine was my protector. When Tim tried to boss me around, she intervened. It felt like I finally had the older sister I had always wished for.

Having Jeannine around was suddenly like having my own Wonder Woman on my side. Needless to say, my affection for Jeannine was profound. I loved her! I loved how she looked out for me. Over time, I've come to understand that she was an extraordinary individual who graced our lives for multiple reasons, almost like an angel walking among us.

However, Jeannine was not without baggage. She had issues, many of them quite serious. Her biological parents were drug addicts. All ten of their children were split up in different foster homes. In her young life, she'd been abandoned, abused, and shopped around in the Chicago Foster Care System.

Before long, Jeannine and Mom would argue, and she'd run away for a few days. She did that a lot, and every time she ran away, I was afraid I would never see her again. Her abandonment fears quickly became mine as well. But she always came back. Even after the loudest arguments, Jeannine always came back.

With her around, things were better. I had Grammy and now Jeannine. I was beginning to feel indestructible as long as they were on my side. But even in my young mind, I always knew there was something greater protecting me.

*I hadn't seen Grammy in years, but there she was, standing on the other side of the room, looking deeply into my eyes, the same uncondi-tional love as always permeating from her being.*

*"Grammy!" I yelled.*

*"I've missed you, Tami," she said.*

*Once again, Grammy came to me in a time of desperation. She was here to save me one more time. Grammy could make everything better. Yes, I do mean EVERYTHING! I knew she could.*

*I'd seen and felt it many times before. She'll just wrap those Grammy arms around me and squeeze all the bad away.*

*"Grammy," I cried. "My baby is sick. She's really sick, and I'm afraid."*

*"I know she is, honey. I know you're scared, too," she said reassuringly.*

*I was crying so loudly, and she put her finger over her mouth and said, "Shhh, be quiet and don't cry. God is aware, and He is ever-present with you."*

*She said nothing more. She just continued to look into my eyes.*

*"Please, Grammy. Make it better, or tell me what I'm supposed to know. You, Grandpa, and my dad are visiting me in my dreams almost daily now, but I don't know what you're trying to tell me. Please! Please! Grammy. I'm so lost and so broken by this."*

*"I love you, Tami."*

*"I love you, too, Grammy."*

*Smiling at me, she opened her arms wide and beckoned me toward her, ready to wrap me once again in her love and safety. My original protector was back, just when I needed her most.*

*"Grammy!" I yelled as I ran across the room toward her, my arms open as wide as hers.*

*If anything could ease my fears, it was getting one of Grammy's soothing hugs. We embraced, and for a millisecond, I thought I felt the love I always felt with Grammy.*

*"My beautiful Tami," she said, giving me another one of her famous squeezes.*

*"Oh, thank you. Thank you for coming back," I said and squeezed back tightly.*

*I had witnessed and experienced it on numerous occasions. She would cover me in her tender Grammy arms, uttering those magical words, "Everything is going to be okay." It was the reassurance I needed at that moment.*

CHAPTER 2

# RATS DON'T RAPE
# —UN-MASKING

*"There are too many quiet ways in which I have
somehow forgotten myself."*

—Alison Malee, poet & author

While our physical dwelling might have been unstable throughout my youth, our mental and emotional abode remained steadfast. I never felt poor growing up. Quite the opposite—I felt a sense of abundance, not in terms of material wealth, which held little meaning, but in every other aspect.

Everyone I loved lived within a half-dozen blocks of wherever my mom, Tim, and I happened to be. We had Grammy's home nearby, offering the comfort of family togetherness, love, and a well-stocked refrigerator.

We had lots of family friends, each with welcoming homes as well. Government cheese turned into the best grilled cheese sandwiches you could imagine. Family was a constant presence, though it came with its own challenges. When I was six or seven years old, an event changed my life permanently. I was innocent and naïve, as children are. My brother, Tim, was nine. My sister Jeannine hadn't joined our family yet.

The preacher's son, who was 15, was spending the night with us for reasons now lost to me. My mom had become friends with his parents through our church, and probably thought having the pastor's teenage son around would positively influence Tim and me. Mom probably thought being a preacher's son meant he was a "good" boy, but her assumption was terribly wrong.

We were having a slumber party—nothing spectacular, just an opportunity to have fun with our friends. Blankets and pillows were on the living room floor, a movie was playing on the TV, and bowls of popcorn were everywhere.

After the movie, the three of us lay on the floor in the dark. As I was lying there, I felt the preacher's son's hand brush up against my leg and come to rest on my outer thigh. He kept it there for a little while, squeezing occasionally, but soon his hand slid from the outside of my leg to the inside, then back up, finally coming to rest on the area Mom called my "private parts." He began to gently rub that area, and I remember thinking it felt kind of good, comfortable even.

At one point, he took my hand and guided it to his private parts, which I remember felt oddly solid. As a little kid, I'd innocently seen private parts before, like accidentally walking in on someone using the restroom, but this one was different. *It felt weird,* I thought, but at the same time, not scary or uncomfortable. The preacher's son pushed my hand further into him. I could tell he enjoyed it, so I didn't pull back. In my young mind, I believed that it would have seemed rude. He continued to grind my hand into his pubic area for some time as I lay there, looking at the ceiling and wondering what in the world was going on. After a few minutes, he grunted, let go of my hand, rolled away, and quickly fell asleep.

In the morning, he acted like nothing had happened. We woke up, had a little breakfast Mom made, and he went back to his house.

Nothing else happened, and I didn't tell anyone about it. Unfortunately, it would not be my only experience with sexual abuse.

A few years later, Jeannine had been placed with another family, and we were now living in a new home, next door to Grammy and Grandpa. I loved living back in my old neighborhood with my aunts, uncles, and cousins all within a one-block radius. Unfortunately, we soon discovered our home was overrun with mice and rats. It was like the rodents ran the show. They came out when they wanted to. They were fearless and bold, scurrying behind the walls and through our rooms. They owned the home we were renting.

Tim and I had our own bedrooms, and for some reason, the rodents liked my room better. They congregated there. I could hear them shuffling across the floor in the dark. If I turned on the light suddenly, they'd disperse quickly into the cracks in the walls or little holes like they were playing hide and seek, and I was "it."

One night, a male family member who was in town spent the night at our place. Our family guest was in a sleeping bag on the floor in Tim's room. On that particular night, the rats got so bad that I was scared to death. I got up, knocked on my brother's door, and asked if I could sleep on the top bunk. He said, "Yes." Reassured, I crawled up the ladder and went to sleep.

In the middle of the night, I felt something touching me, much in the same way the preacher's son had. I instantly froze—what should I do? Just as quickly as that thought registered in my mind, this man was on top of me. His penis was now firm, just like the preacher's son had been. He pushed himself onto me and tried to penetrate. It hurt terribly, but I thought if I yelled, my brother would wake up. Instead, I let it happen. I didn't know what else to do.

My mind raced with thoughts that if Jeannine were still here, she would've certainly harmed him before he had a chance to harm me. As a matter of fact, he would've never gotten close enough to me if Jeannine were still here. I cried myself to sleep that night without ever making a sound, and I never told anyone. Part of my tears were from the trauma I'd just experienced; the other part was grief-stricken tears from missing my big sister. This is when I first learned how to silence my voice and hide deep within myself. This was also when extreme fear became a part of my life, and I no longer felt safe.

The next morning, Mom came into the room and looked at Tim, me, and our guest on the floor. She must've discerned something was off because she frowned at the scene and put an end to me ever leaving my room again.

"You're not sleeping here anymore, Tami. You sleep in your own damn room. Do you hear me?"

I was relegated back to the rodents. It was fine by me. The rats were safer. Rats don't rape.

As I matured, my life became increasingly more complicated, especially when my mom's boyfriend moved in with us.

Why my mom dated this guy, I will never know. If I could recall his name today, which I can't, I wouldn't even dignify it with a mention in this book. He was a creep, no doubt, but at this point in my life, I simply pray for the salvation of his soul as I know he has passed.

As an eleven-year-old, I was allowed to cook my favorite breakfast, which was pancakes. I had become a highly proficient cook as far as pancakes went, an expert at mixing the batter and eggs and milk, buttering the skillet, and, most importantly, flipping. A pancake professional must be a world-class flipper, which I was.

One quiet morning, I was alone in the kitchen making pancakes while Mom's boyfriend was in the next room on the sofa watching TV. It was about flip-time. The batter was getting bubbly, and I was about to do my thing when a mouse darted suddenly across the stove in front of me, nearly landing in the hot skillet with my prized pancakes.

I screamed.

"A mouse!" I yelled and ran away from the stove. "Help! Mouse!"

I backed away from the stove, frightened, too scared to shoo the mouse away. It remained there, sitting right by the pancakes.

"Help, please, there's a mouse on the stove!" I screamed again.

The pancakes started to burn.

I was standing there, staring at the mouse and trying to think of what to do, when I heard—

"WHAT THE FUCK ARE YOU DOING, BITCH?!"

My pleas had obviously interrupted whatever the creep was doing. He was right in my face. I pointed meekly to the mouse and asked him to help.

"SHUT THE FUCK UP AND LEAVE ME ALONE."

It was the first time in my life that that type of language had been directed at me. It was devastating to be spoken to that way. I began to cry.

"STOP FUCKIN' CRYING AND TAKE CARE OF THOSE PANCAKES."

I returned obediently to the stove, which was now mouse-free. The creep's screaming must have scared it as much as it did me. I turned off the fire below the skillet. One side of the pancakes was charcoal black, and the other still had runny yellow batter—a gross concoction.

I picked up the skillet, carried it toward the kitchen trash can, tilted it toward the garbage, and made the first motions to scrape the ruined breakfast from the pan into the refuse.

"WHAT ARE YOU DOING? YOU'RE NOT GOING TO WASTE FUCKIN' FOOD!"

He was staring at me, daring me to scrape a scrap of pancake into the trash. I instinctively knew if as much as a morsel fell into the garbage can, he would explode on me. I averted my eyes from his, carried the skillet back to the stove, and with a spatula, I transferred the burnt gooey gobs of would-be pancakes onto a plate.

He was still standing there, watching me.

"NOW SIT DOWN AND EAT."

The rage in his voice lingered even as he returned to the couch. I sat at the kitchen table and wept into my pancakes. I reverted inward even more with each tear that fell. I had never been spoken to like that before, but it wouldn't be the last time.

There were several instances like that during the creep's stay with us. Today, they call it verbal abuse, which indeed it was, but as a little girl, such behavior from a grown man was terrifying when it was directed my way.

On another day, I was outside our home playing with my slightly younger cousins, Dana and Darin, the children of my mom's younger sister. They lived next door with Grammy, and we were very close. It was summer and hot. After a while, I broke away from the others for a quick trip inside for a cold drink and a restroom break.

As I tried to pass through the house to our powder room, I almost tripped over a large lump on the floor. Looking down, I realized it was the creep. He was face down, motionless.

I thought he was dead.

Once again, I screamed out of fright. I ran out of our house and across the street to Grammy's.

"Grammy, come quick!" I said, crying and gasping and afraid. "He's dead! He's dead!"

Grammy bolted from her chair and, as fast as she could, hurried out of her house, across the street, and into our place.

"Get up," Grammy said to the creep on the floor, shaking him awake. "Get up."

He made some weird noise, stirred a bit, and then sat up.

"He's drunk," Grammy said. She directed a few choice words his way, turned, and left. She and Grandpa didn't like him anyway.

I stood there staring at him. As much as I detested him, I was glad I hadn't walked in on a corpse in our powder room.

"YOU FUCKIN BITCH, HOW DARE YOU!" he screamed at me. "WHY'D YOU BRING THAT NOSY-ASS WOMAN OVER HERE?"

*"I thought you might have been dead,"* I remember thinking, although I don't think I said it out loud. I was petrified!

"MIND YOUR OWN BUSINESS, YOU LITTLE SHIT!" he said before laying back down on the floor.

Two weeks later, on a day when the creep was at work, with the quiet rage that was now not only brewing but boiling inside of me, I strolled solo into the second-floor master bedroom he shared with Mom.

Very calmly, I began to remove his things—first from the drawers and then from the closet. When every one of his personal items—clothes, toiletries, and whatever looked like it was his and not Mom's—was in a pile on the bed, I opened the nearby window and, item by item, began tossing *everything* he owned onto the front lawn below.

To this day, I still don't know what came over me, but I was furious, filled with and fueled by what felt like a demon-like rage inside me. All I knew was I saw red, and he was going to pay. This act of defiance had been long in the making! It was birthed from everything that I had endured, beginning with the sexual molestation I'd suffered through, the unaddressed and repressed trauma and grief from my younger years, and everything else to that point. When I was finished, not a scintilla of his personal effects or any hint of his existence remained inside our rat-infested home.

I walked back downstairs into the living room, had a seat, and waited for the creep to come home. This had to have been an out-of-body experience because I had NO FEAR or even a thought or care of the repercussions of my actions. I was dangerous at that very moment!

When he walked through the door, he'd already seen the mess of his stuff in the yard outside. So had our family, neighbors, and various passersby. I was dangerously ready for fireworks! Battle ready with everything within me!

His eyes met mine when he entered the living room, but this time, I kept the stare. I was a fifth-grade girl who'd had enough, and I think he could tell. The fury in my eyes told him the slightest provocation—even thinking the word "bitch"—would trigger a cataclysmic reaction from me. I was seriously not even scared of what his reaction would be. I simply stared at him with fiery internal rage, *welcoming* his next move.

He looked away.

That night, after my mom got home from work, a terrible fight ensued between them. Shortly thereafter, the creep moved out, and I've never seen him again.

Score one for the little girl.

There is something in life I call the cycle of grief.

For me, it began at a pitifully young age with the abuses I've detailed: sexual, verbal, and emotional. Such exploitation cuts *deeply* into a person's soul; it bleeds out and then seemingly heals until you realize it hasn't.

The events of my childhood recounted on these pages happened decades ago, but the wounds seem fresh still, as if the abuse and mental anguish it caused happened just this afternoon.

You can try to move on. Some people even believe that you'll grow out of it if you give it time. Unfortunately, it is not that simple; you often simply can't or won't. Such abuse at an early age gets deeply internalized; it becomes part of your circulatory system.

Not to be dismissive of the incidents involving the preacher's son, my family member, or the creep. Each of those incidents damaged me deeply and almost permanently. I see the scars today from the cuts back then, but looking back, the sexual, mental, and verbal abuse was *nothing* compared to what was to come. As traumatic as these events were, they would pale in comparison to what would come in the next seasons of my life.

# CHAPTER 3

# THE DIAGNOSIS
# THAT STOLE EVERYTHING

*"I've found that if I pray for God to move a mountain,*
*I must be prepared to wake up next to a shovel."*

–Unknown

Happiness can be like a foster home. You never know when the good times will end. This became real once Jeannine became part of our family. In her, I gained a best friend and protector, second to Tim, of course. She was an older sister I could look up to, a female lead I could easily follow.

For good reasons, Jeannine trusted few people. Up until now, it had been a matter of survival for her. She felt as if her home today could disappear tomorrow. She feared abandonment like no young person should. She had suffered different forms of abuse, too, a fate all too common for many foster children.

Jeannine enjoyed going to church with us. She seemed happy and content in that environment. Church seemed to bring a certain peace to her soul. She would enjoy and participate in our youth activities. She enjoyed the doting of the Church Mothers. For me, time and space would often overlap, stop, pause, or even seem like they weren't in chronological order. At seven years old, I remember feeling happy when I saw Jeannine happy.

One day, Jeannine, who had just turned fifteen, complained about a sore throat, saying it was hard to swallow. Probably nothing, my mom thought at first, perhaps strep. Kids pass around strep at school like they do a football at recess. But her sore throat didn't go away. In fact, the pain continued unabated for a few days until Mom could feel a lump in her esophagus, a little bump on her windpipe, I remember her saying.

Mom took Jeannine to our pediatrician, who examined her throat and referred her to a specialist, who referred her to another specialist, who referred her to another. Each doctor said something was wrong, but they couldn't pinpoint exactly what. More tests were always required.

We finally ended up one afternoon at Loyola University Medical Center, a widely respected hospital in Chicago's western suburbs that is perennially ranked among the best in the nation. By this time, Jeannine was in unrelenting pain.

She sat on the exam table as the doctor, an ear, nose, and throat specialist, silently examined her charts and X-rays. He shook his head nearly imperceptibly as he read.

"Okay, let's have a look here," the doctor said to Jeannine. "Now open wide and say aah."

My sister did as he instructed her to do and opened wide.

The doctor peered into Jeannine's mouth and down her throat. He paused, then did it again. He turned away to read the accompanying paperwork a second time, a look of concern on his face. He returned to face Jeannine.

"One more look. Open wide again," he said. She did.

The doctor turned off and put down his examination light. He stepped away from Jeannine and turned slowly to my mother.

"She's got cancer," he said to Mom.

Jeannine sat there, her face blank and expressionless.

"He didn't even touch her," I remember hearing my mom tell family and friends of the diagnosis. "He just took another look and said, 'She's got cancer,' and that was that."

That was that.

Jeannine moved to another foster home not long after getting the news, to another family with a two-parent home where she would get more individual attention during her cancer battle. I understood she needed to move on, but it was difficult to watch her move out. I cried for the loss of my sister. I cried out of fear for her and me.

Living with the new family, Jeannine underwent throat surgery on two different occasions to remove cancerous tumors. Her new foster mother, Kathy, was very good about keeping us in the loop. Jeannine would call and talk with me occasionally, joking around and always making my day. God, I missed her, but even at a young age, I realized she was probably better off with Kathy's family, especially as she fought this disease. I loved Jeannine and wanted the best for her.

Jeannine was a week shy of her sixteenth birthday when we got the call. It was Kathy. Mom listened and nodded. She said she understood. She thanked Kathy, who had become a friend of hers. She hung up.

"Jeannine passed away," my mom said. She didn't say anything else.

My body went numb. It seemed like suddenly I was in a bad dream. I'd lost my protector. I'd lost my big sister. It didn't seem possible. My mom held me as I cried. My brother cried, too. He and Jeannine had fought like brothers and sisters do, but he loved her as we all did.

Days later, we found ourselves in a Chicago funeral home. In front of us, Jeannine lay there, beautiful and peaceful, in a lovely peach-colored chiffon dress and headwrap as she'd lost her hair due to the chemo. I stared into her casket, dazed, the situation surreal.

"Come with me," my mom said, her words puncturing my thoughts. "We need to go next door."

"Why?" I asked.

"Just come with me."

We walked down a long hallway. I didn't know why we'd leave my sister to visit a stranger's wake, but within a minute, I was standing in front of another deceased person. This one was a young man who was not much older than Jeannine.

"This is Jeannine's brother," Mom said, looking down at the body before us. I'd never seen him before. He had been killed a few days prior, right around the time of Jeannine's passing. The same funeral home was handling his arrangements. Within a few hours, Jeannine's biological siblings had permanently lost two members of their family.

In the days following my sister's funeral, we tried to resume life as usual. Nobody talked about our loss. The name Jeannine came up seldomly. Certainly, nobody asked about my feelings or how I was processing such an upsetting event.

Again, there were no counselors readily available for consultation. We were expected to buck up, move forward, and get busy with something else to keep the trauma tamped down.

But it had become part of my foundation. This is how I learned to process grief and trauma—I didn't. I simply absorbed it and resumed my day-to-day life.

Weeks later, while sitting in a circle at school one day, playing a game, I remember thinking, *I'm different,* and feeling it for the first time.

My eyes made their way around the circle, stopping on every face of every classmate, most of them smiling and laughing, all of them engaged in the silly game we were playing. Their faces seemed so joyful, cherubic, and innocent. I don't know what my face looked like to them, but inside, I felt anything but happy.

As a matter of fact, I didn't feel anything but very different, alone, out of place, and unable to identify with any of the kids in my class. I didn't know why I wasn't one of the happy ones, but I knew in my spirit even then that it was my truth.

There were so many reasons that could have contributed to my unhappiness. My sister Jeannine had died, and I didn't know how to process or grieve her loss. Maybe it was because of what the preacher's son had done that evening, not so long before, or how I'd wished I'd fought off the family member as he'd tried to penetrate me. It could be because of the stinging verbal abuse hurled at me by my mother's boyfriend. Another reason could be that we have jumped from home to home, seldom having a fixed address for more than a school year. Or maybe it was a combination of all the trauma I had experienced. There were so many unanswered questions.

As I got older and now, as I look back, I understand that unaddressed trauma doesn't simply go away. One of the most profound explanations of this that connects with me very deeply is something I heard Iyanla Vanzant say years ago: "Feelings buried alive don't die. They fester. They corrupt. They explode … and manifest into other things and in other ways. And that fear or that upset or that anger or that whatever it is, it'll turn into something inside of you. So you want to get it out."[1]

Whatever it was, it had won. By now, I was a different creature from those school kids playing in the circle. I knew it. I felt it within me, even if I couldn't articulate it, a seething, quiet rage, an emotion no young girl should ever know or feel.

My deep-rooted anger would manifest itself in various forms.

In church, I remember staring at the pulpit and the large cross that projected behind it, believing little of what was being said by the pastor up front, all this nonsense about caring for your neighbor. *Some neighbors I had,* I thought. One of them had sexually assaulted me. As for brotherly love, it was drivel, too. When the preacher talked about turning the other cheek, I could focus only on how much I hated my mother's boyfriend. As for heaven, the place where everyone said Jeannine now resided with Jesus, if it was indeed real, it couldn't come soon enough for me.

I was already a bitter woman.

While I sat stewing at church, sitting by myself and not participating with the others in the Bible story we were being taught, my godfather approached me. Next to my grandfather and my dad, Richmond, he was the most significant male influence in my young life. He was another safe space for me.

He was a man of the church. He'd been with me during my baptism. Before a church full of witnesses, he committed to be there for me throughout my life. He was a deacon and respected elder. I knew him to be a good and kind man.

"Oh my, Tami, what has happened to you?" he asked out of genuine concern. "Why do you have all this rage inside of you?"

---

[1] Iyanla Vanzant, interview with Michel Martin, *Tell Me More*, NPR, March 2014, https://www.azquotes.com/quote/1209717.

It shocked me for him to say that. That he actually saw me. That I wasn't as invisible as I'd thought I was.

He said he could see anger and rage on my face, feel it in my body language, and see it in the way I seemed so indifferent to the games the other Sunday School kids played.

"What has happened to you, Tami?" he asked again.

I looked away, nonresponsive, into an empty distance. My nonanswer, though, wouldn't suffice. He walked out and then returned with my mom. He tried to talk quietly, but his voice carried across the auditorium.

"Something is wrong with Tami," he said to my mom. "She's a kid. She's a baby. Why does she have all this rage inside her?"

He was fishing for answers, but my mother provided none. In fact, she dismissed him by saying something like, "Oh, she's fine," or "Tami's just having a bad day."

But my godfather knew differently, and so did I.

Yes, there was rage boiling inside of me. There were sexual feelings, too, even if I was too young to call it that. There was fear of abandonment. I had lost my sister, first to another home and then to death. I felt like there was little permanence in my life. Inside my head, it often felt like an eternal hurricane, a chaos that never quite ended; instead, it just shifted in another destructive direction—none of which I could understand or rectify.

"Oh, Tami's all right," my mom repeated. "She's probably a little tired or has an attitude today."

And that was the end of that. My godfather never questioned my mom again. And the rage inside me continued to fester.

After my mom's boyfriend moved out and Jeannine passed away, things began to change between my mom and me. A chasm grew between us, one that I feel never fully healed. In my young, rage-filled mind, I believed she resented me, and I reverted inward.

The gulf between us widened even more in my early teens when I became ill.

I began to suffer from severe stomach pains, the kind that had me doubled over, writhing on the floor. The pain always arrived suddenly and intensely but then left as quickly as it had come. At first, Mom didn't seem to believe me, or at least thought I was overdramatizing the hurt. I wasn't.

When the pain wouldn't subside, Mom relented and took me to see our doctor. He couldn't find anything out of the ordinary, so he referred us to another doctor, who referred us to another—the same pattern that preceded Jeannine's diagnosis and death. I remember thinking I was going to die just as she had. *Soon, I'd join Jeannine in a beautiful place free from all the bad things I felt had shaped my young life,* I thought.

One day, I was seeing a specialist who was examining my stomach. He was a nice doctor who tried to put me at ease. He told me he was going to look down my throat and into my belly. He held a scope with a light at the end of it, a camera he called it, and said it would take pictures inside my stomach that would help him help me.

I lay back on the examination table. The doctor dimmed the lights and told me to say "Aah," just as Jeannine's doctor had requested she do some months earlier. *That's when it all went bad for her,* I thought.

As the doctor stood over me and began to look into my mouth, I freaked out. Totally freaked. It wasn't because of the lighted scope or the memory of my sister's experience, either. The fact that a man was looming over me and peering down unnerved me.

I rose and tried to get away.

"No. No," I yelled, determined he was going to try to force himself upon me. "Let me go! Let me out of here!"

The doctor stepped back. Clearly, he was shocked.

"But, honey, we just need to—"

"No!" I screamed.

Triggered thoughts of the pastor's son, my family member's heavy body on mine, and the roar of my mother's boyfriend directing his anger at me all plagued me at once.

"No!" I said as I jumped off the exam table. I would not be examined by a male.

My stomach pain continued until I was later hospitalized, a situation that only made me feel more isolated from my mom. They had admitted me for a few days to run several tests. I continued complaining about the pain, and the doctors suggested a comprehensive scrutiny of my insides. Something was obviously causing the discomfort, but even medical specialists couldn't pinpoint it.

During my stay, my mom barely came to visit. She was working three jobs by this point and simply didn't have the time to see me every day. My roommate in the hospital was a nice girl named Lisa. I noticed how Lisa's parents barely left her side. They seemed to have brought her presents each day. There were beautiful flowers decorating her side of the room. For Lisa, there was constant activity that seemed endless, including playing board games, watching her favorite cartoons, and visiting with a collection of relatives and friends. Eventually, Lisa's parents began bringing me gifts as well. They obviously realized I had no visitors, so they took pity on me.

One day, my mom called. She asked how I was feeling, so I told her.

"Mom, I wish you could be here," I said. It was a simple, innocent request.

She blew up.

"YOU KNOW I'M WORKING," she screamed into the receiver. "I'M TRYING TO MAKE ENDS MEET AND DON'T NEED TO HEAR THIS STUFF FROM YOU."

After hanging up, I rolled over on my side, away from Lisa and her family, tears running down my cheeks and onto my hospital gown. I remember feeling the most alone I'd ever felt.

I never brought it up again, and she did visit sparingly, as much as she could.

In a couple of days, after the many tests the doctors conducted failed to show anything abnormal, I was released from the hospital. Back in the cycle.

The instability of my young existence was confusing and angering, but ironically, I never had stomach pains again, which led me to believe it was psychosomatic. Perhaps it was my way of screaming in vain for love and attention.

Things continued to get worse with Mom and me. Not that she ever said this to me, but I always felt like I was a burden to her.

She would take my brother back-to-school shopping, spending hundreds of dollars on him in new clothes, shoes, and the coolest school supplies. They would leave for a long afternoon, returning happy and carrying numerous shopping bags.

When I gently reminded Mom that my school year was starting up, too, she snapped.

"What do you want from me? I'm doing the best I can," she yelled.

In hindsight, I knew it wasn't me. It was the stress of the situation and maybe even the guilt she carried. My dad was very present in my life. In all honesty, he ensured I was always well taken care of. He'd show up when he said he would and made sure I had new clothes, shoes, and any other needs met.

My brother's dad, on the other hand, was the polar opposite, which deeply affected Tim. Mom was simply trying to fill the gap for him by overcompensating for it. She was a nurturer doing what nurturers do, but I didn't realize that it made me feel like I was on the outside looking in on their relationship. They always seemed to have a good and close relationship, and then there was me.

I learned not to ask for much from her; I didn't want to cause her additional anger or stress. If my dad didn't get it for me, I resorted to stealing it or simply going without it.

Although my stomach pain, real or imagined, never returned, neither did my childhood innocence and wonderment. In my short time on earth, I'd seen and experienced more trauma than young ladies three times my age. It had affected my personality, too, and not in a good way.

I became a thief and a schoolyard bully, the type of person Jeannine had always protected me against.

There was a particular little girl I liked to pick on. She was smaller and more sensitive than me, so I could make her cry. It oddly made me feel better about my life when she did.

As was my pattern, each day I'd approach her. Sometimes, in the hallway or on the playground—regardless of where, the result was always the same—I'd smack her in the face.

Not one hard smack, but several, until she was a screaming, wailing mess. Being small and relatively defenseless, she was an easy target.

That little girl learned to fear the school bell and leaving the safety of her classroom. She knew I'd be waiting for her to dish out a painful, unjustified beating. The other kids got a kick out of it, and it made me feel part of their gang, which I really wasn't.

I was becoming the person I'd always feared, and I was barely past adolescence. Little did I know, even then, that I was on a journey—a journey to freedom.

# CHAPTER 4

# ZIPLOC BAG

*"If you run into the little girl I used to be, let her know that everything she suffered through was well worth the investment of her heart and broken soul. That the woman she is today is the woman she needed then."*

—Tami Franklin

I was in the seventh or eighth grade when I really got to know my dad. It felt good to have the comfort and safety of him as my dad.

He would stop by our home, pick me up, and we'd drive over to his place. His wife, Geraldine, was always good to me. She made me feel at home, which was quite a feat back then.

Geraldine had two daughters, Anne, who was eight years older than me, the same age as Jeannine would have been had she lived, and Yolanda, who was only a year older than me. Yolanda and I became what I consider to be good friends. She was funny and fun to be around.

My dad's family had something ours always lacked: stability. Inside those walls, it felt comfortable. There was a sense of security, a sense of peace and permanence. I remember that although I initially resented the structure of my dad's home, I soon began craving the security and safety I felt there.

There were family dinners almost every night. There was homework time. There were holidays planned and celebrated. There was conversation, love, and laughter. Lots of laughter. It felt the way I'd always imagined a family should feel.

Dad's house was built on a foundation; it was something I honestly hadn't directly experienced before. Sure, I indirectly experienced that through Grammy and Grandpa's home and my aunts' and uncles' homes, but it was never my direct experience.

My dad wanted me to move in with them. He was upfront about this. He asked me a couple of times to consider it. I believe he knew the atmosphere I breathed daily and the struggles my home life presented. He thought I'd be better off living with him, Geraldine, and the girls, but I wasn't ready for such a leap. I loved Mom and Tim, even if our existence together was often complicated, and as hard as things often were, they were the family I knew best.

If I'm being fully transparent, I felt sorry for my mom and didn't want to sadden her by choosing to live with my dad. I carried that emotional burden, and quite honestly, being well aware of that internal struggle, she seemed to find her own level of comfort in it.

Truthfully, I think my mom was afraid to lose me to my dad. I wasn't ready to even consider leaving them permanently, though. I enjoyed spending a night or two at Dad's house, but I would begin to feel panicked when I had been away from my mom and Tim for too long.

Back in Grammy's neighborhood, I was becoming popular with the boys, but not in the way you might think.

At twelve years old, I could outrun almost any boy around. We would race through the street, and I'd win. We'd play basketball, and I could more than hold my own, thanks to Tim. I could catch, dribble, and pass a basketball as well as any guy.

I quickly realized there was something else remarkable about hanging out with boys my age, something I had never experienced with girls: they were drama-free. Unless we were arguing over a foul in hoops or whether a catch was inbounds, playing with boys was remarkably easy and fun.

With the boys, they only cared about how good I was and if I'd be able to help them win if they picked me for their team. The game was about the game.

With girls, things were much different. There were cliques and backstabs, muttered comments, one-ups, and catty cutdowns. The neighborhood girls, I learned, resented me for being popular with the boys and for being asked to play with them when the other girls weren't.

But I was nevertheless a girl, and naturally, I wanted to hang with the girls, too. But it wasn't as easy as that, not with the girls in that neighborhood.

I was offered a proposal. I can't remember which girl informed me of it, but it had apparently been a group decision.

"If you want to be friends with us," said one of the girls, "You aren't allowed to even look at the boys for 90 days."

It sounded like a terrible deal even then. I mean, 90 days is an entire season. I couldn't race the boys or play basketball or dodgeball or anything else. Playing with the boys accounted for much of my day.

"You're not allowed to talk to them, either," said another girl. The rest nodded in agreement.

"It's us or the boys," a third girl added. "Your choice, Tami."

"Okay," I said reluctantly. I agreed to stay away from the boys, but I didn't understand why. It didn't make sense why I couldn't play with everyone.

The treaty I'd been coerced into accepting, however, didn't last long. A few days later, a kickball game was brewing, and the boys were assembling talent. They asked me to play—and I automatically joined in. It was what I did. I was never really a girly girl anyway. It was a great game, too, I recall even now, and it seemed to last for most of that hot summer afternoon.

When it was over, I think my team won, but it didn't matter because as I walked back to Grammy's home, I ran into a wall of little women. It seems they'd been watching the kickball game from afar.

Unlike the boys, the girls weren't impressed with my performance.

"We watched you break your promise. You're a fake, a phony, and a hoe," said one of the girls.

"You are OUT! You're DONE playing with us. FOR-EVER!" another one chimed in.

"She's probably sleeping with all of them," quipped a third. All the girls descended into mean, spiteful laughter, turned, and walked away.

"DONE," one of them repeated for good measure.

They meant it. I never played with them again. It hurt, but in a way, it was also a relief. I cried that night, but the next morning, I left my home early for Grammy's neighborhood, carrying a basketball, and went out to find a game.

That same year, my mother's first cousin, Donald, arrived in town for a visit. Donald was Mom's age or a little older. A few years earlier, he had moved from Maywood to Los Angeles. I remember everyone making a huge deal about the fact that Donald was back in town, thinking he was living the glamorous life in L.A. and had selflessly returned home for a spell to grace us with his presence.

Donald seemed to like the attention, and he played up the whole California thing—swimming pools, movie stars, you know—every time he visited our home, which all of a sudden was frequently. He was one of my mom's favorite cousins, and they were getting reacquainted.

It was an early weekday, a little before noon, and Mom was still at work when Donald came to visit. I was home alone, watching TV, and I let him in when he knocked.

"My mom will be home later this evening," I told him, less interested in visiting with Donald than I was in returning to my show.

He took a seat on the living room sofa. I returned to my place on the floor in front of a cartoon. I was lying on my belly in front of the television, my chest propped up by a throw pillow, eating a bowl of cereal in my usual at-home attire—a long T-shirt and little else.

Donald began talking to me, about what I don't exactly recall. I just remember it was annoying. I was trying to watch the program, but he kept talking and talking, rambling on about nothing of interest to me.

At one point, he addressed me directly.

"Hey, Tami, look here," he said.

I turned away from the TV and back toward him. Donald was sitting on the couch, his pants unzipped, exposing himself to me.

I saw what he obviously wanted me to see, then quickly looked away. He continued to sit there with an odd, self-satisfied look on his face. Donald wasn't the preacher's son or my other family member, who were both young. He was a grown man.

I felt sick, then panicked. *Not again!* I thought as I got up quickly and walked to my bedroom, closing the door behind me, putting on a pair of pants, and sitting motionless on the edge of my bed for what seemed like hours. I prayed he wouldn't come into the room. I asked Jesus to keep him away from me.

After a few minutes, I heard his footsteps walk across our living room floor and out the front door. He never tried to enter my room, and I never saw Donald again.

The Donald story reminds me of the end of my fifth-grade year when we had to move once more.

Our apartment building had been sold to someone else, and we were only given short notice to move out. Mom found us a two-story duplex about seven blocks away, but it was in a different school district, so I had to switch schools again, too.

It was at this point, the start of middle school years, that my grades began to suffer. I'd always been an A or B student at my other schools, a permanent name on the honor roll. My teachers had always commended me for my academic achievement, and it was this rare praise I cherished and internalized. I'd always felt like an intelligent girl when my teachers affirmed me this way.

Something happened at my new school, though, something odd and uncomfortable. I began to struggle.

At first, my test scores were not noticeably lower. Then, as the semester grades rolled in, my traditional As and Bs disappeared, replaced with Cs or worse.

The repeated incidents of sexual and verbal abuse, the general dysfunction and chaos of my home life, the self-esteem issues of my bad acne at the time, and the nasty comments kids made about it all caught up to me at once.

I withdrew completely. First from schoolwork, then from the outside world. I began to ditch school, acting as if I were sick, to get out of attending my classes.

It was a surprisingly easy thing to do, I discovered, at least in my home. Mom was too busy working to notice how this was becoming a huge problem. On many mornings, I'd fake a stomach ache, a headache, the flu, or anything I thought I could act my way through. My mom would simply call the school and inform them of my illness. They'd send homework home, but I'd just ignore it.

Toward the end of the academic year, however, I got a rude awakening. The principal called my mom and, referring to school absences that now numbered in the dozens, broke the jarring news.

"You've got to withdraw Tami from this school and send her somewhere else," she said without mincing words. "She's not going to pass the seventh grade at this school."

To her credit, Mom acted quickly. She sent me back to an old school I'd attended before. It was close to Grammy's house, so I visited there before and after school again. It was also brimming with old friends I hadn't seen in a while. For a place so old and familiar, it seemed so new and boundless.

Almost immediately, my schoolwork improved. In fact, I began to excel again.

Before this, I'd been called dumb too many times to count in my past by people across the spectrum of my life. Fool. Stupid. Retard. They were all hurled my way. After a while, I think

I began to believe it. That is, until Mr. Mobley called me something else.

"Jackson, you're a *writer*," he said to me one morning.

Mr. Mobley was passing back graded essays. Mine was marked with a large red "A+."

He paused mid-aisle as he handed me my paper. I could tell he wasn't joking around.

"You are a writer. You can write, Jackson (as he called me). Do you understand what I'm saying? You've got *talent*. Real talent," he said.

Mr. Mobley referred to my writing ability in front of the class. He read my paper out loud and used my sentences or paragraphs to illustrate his points about composition. It felt like the most wonderful thing in the world.

"Jackson has it together, class," I recall him saying one day. "Try to write your papers like she writes hers."

Back in my old school, with my newfound writing talent on display, courtesy of Mr. Mobley, I became something I'd never been before. I became popular among my peers. My grades improved. My self-esteem soared. I think even most of my acne went away.

The remainder of middle school was the best time of my school days.

I had the typical high school crushes on famous people. Mine was with Michael Jackson. I was totally in love with him.

Of course, every other girl in America was in love with Michael, too. Only my name was Jackson, just like his, which would make things very easy for Michael and me when it was time for us to be married. Of all the girls in the world, I felt I sincerely had the best shot of landing Michael.

This was the "Thriller" era, and I went nowhere without my Michael Jackson Members Only jacket, bright red, with a dozen zippers and hundreds of buttons adorning it. I'd asked my family and friends to kindly refer to me as Mrs. Jackson so that they'd be in practice when our love was officially sealed.

High school was different, though. Much different from my glorious middle school years. As much as I'd recovered my academic footing in middle school, I lost it again when I entered ninth grade.

In the classroom, I couldn't concentrate. I don't know if it was the stress I always seemed to be battling or the fact that I suffered from an undiagnosed form of ADD. My grades began to slip again. In my social life, I felt distant, unable to join in entirely with the happy, joking classmates who surrounded me. My self-esteem began to plummet. When I'd walk the hallways, upper-level students would knock my books to the floor.

I began skipping school again, this time not staying home but hanging out with other kids who were also ditching classes. I began to smoke weed, drink alcohol, and have sex regularly.

By my sophomore year, I was pregnant and completely numbed out.

*I can't tell my mom*, I thought, *she'll kill me*. Telling my dad was out of the question, too. Jeannine was dead. Tim was away at college by this point and would only tell Mom, and I knew Grammy would have a heart attack.

Horrified, confused, and without anyone in whom to confide, I was determined to somehow, some way, lose the baby that was growing inside me. I tried taking lots of pills, but they were only aspirin. I thought if I did a bunch of sit-ups, the pregnancy would go away. I even tried punching myself in the stomach, as terrible as that sounds.

I was a lost, naïve little girl who was about to become a mother. I retreated into my mind, not saying anything to anyone, quietly praying it would just go away.

A few weeks into my pregnancy, I miscarried the baby. I was sitting on the toilet when the embryo passed from within me. It made a kerplunk as it hit the water. I unconsciously reached into the toilet bowl and retrieved it, dried it off, put it in a Ziploc bag, and put the bag in my top dresser drawer.

I cried. I asked for forgiveness from God. And I began to bleed.

For two days, I bled profusely until I summoned the courage to call my mom. She was at work as usual. I explained I was bleeding very badly and that I needed to go to the hospital.

"When was your last period?" she asked, along with what seemed like a million other questions.

She hung up and called an older cousin of mine, a woman who was always judgmental toward me. She picked me up and drove me to the hospital. While driving there, she too grilled me by asking invasive questions like, "When was your last period?" and "Are you having sex?"

Knowing that my business would've quickly spread through the family and network of friends, church members, and others, I was evasively calculated with my answers and acted as if I had no clue what was wrong. The emergency room curb couldn't appear quickly enough. She pulled up, waited for me to get out, and simply drove away.

Four hours later, after the doctor and nurses had stopped the bleeding, I confessed to them about my miscarriage two days earlier. My mom arrived at the hospital. One of the attendants explained the circumstances that had brought me to them. I had no words for my mom. No explanation. I was cold-hearted and grieving.

"How could this happen?!" she screamed. "When did this happen?! Who did this to you?!"

I stared silently at the examination room floor. I would let my mom throw her fit, as I knew she would. I'd let her curse my name, as she'd done before. I sat there hollow, empty, the shell of a now 15-year-old girl on the outside, a vacuous nothing on the inside.

"I'm going to call your dad," she said, shocking me into action.

"Please don't call him," I cried.

I knew my dad would demand immediate changes to my life, starting with the mandate that I would have to move in with him. My dad, I knew from our time together, was no-nonsense. He provided the discipline, structure, and order I knew I desperately needed but didn't want. Life in my dad's house would drastically change the life of partying, drinking, and chilling with friends, which I'd become accustomed to as a way to further numb the deep pain I lived with but had no words for. There was no way I could live under his roof and by his rules at this point in my life.

"Please, please don't tell my dad," I begged her again.

For once, my mom listened to my plea and didn't call my dad. Surprisingly, she never told him anything about that day. Instead, Mom took me to another doctor, who wrote me a prescription for birth control pills.

And that was that.

There was no further conversation between us about the events that led to my pregnancy. There were no counseling sessions. There wasn't even a suggestion that perhaps I should attend my high school classes more often. Life and the cycle of brokenness continued.

CHAPTER 5

# CATHOLIC SCHOOL

*"There is a beauty in people that only reveals itself when they are free—for who they truly are is often hidden behind what they need to be delivered from."*

–Unknown

Maybe it was because of the prayer breaks we'd take throughout the day, but for some reason, I always liked attending Catholic schools. Before morning classes, we'd collectively send up *Our Fathers* and *Hail Marys*. Maybe it was because of the uniforms they made us wear, which were great equalizers of sorts. When everyone is dressed the same, nobody gets made fun of for their hand-me-down clothes. Maybe it was the structure. Unlike public schools, parochial school teachers were allowed to smack our butts or tap our knuckles, which instilled in us a certain fear, but it also created a certain calm. Deep down, I knew I needed discipline. In fact, I craved it, yet I also denied it. It was indeed a fierce internal battle.

I knew my mom couldn't afford to send me to Catholic school, so I thought, *Maybe Dad can pay for it.* He was always working and made a good living.

Without anyone knowing, I'd arranged to take the placement test for a local but popular Catholic high school. I aced it! I scored high and was offered a slot in the following fall's class. I was ecstatic!

I visited my dad with my acceptance letter from the school. I showed him my score and the official congratulations note from the principal, and, ever so gently, asked Dad if he could possibly pay for my tuition. He said he'd think about it and get back to me.

As the long summer days stretched into August and toward a new school year, I'd still not received confirmation from my dad that he was cool with footing the bill. As the clock ticked, my subtle hints sharpened. Unlike public schools, there was tuition that needed to be paid in advance before the first day of classes.

"I can't send you."

I remember the words exactly. It was a gut-punch of a sentence.

"I'm sorry, Tami. I can't send you to Catholic school."

He never explained why. At this point, I desperately needed the structure of a Catholic school to continue to excel. I wanted to be successful and accomplish something good in my life, and I instinctively knew that I would spiral out of control without the strict culture of Catholic school.

I never asked why. I didn't really want to know. I just absorbed the denial like I did all negative things.

"No, Tami, I just can't do it."

And with those few words, it was over. I'd be attending public school after all, trying to avoid the chaos of the classrooms and hallways or perhaps the chaos in my brain that was begging to explode. I knew I was in trouble, but no one else did.

I told my dad I understood his decision, but I never truly did. I was sad and nearly devastated. I felt like this was my chance at something good to help anchor me in a sense, and now it was suddenly over.

*If I were confined to public school, so be it,* I thought. At first, I was determined to do well no matter what. To really apply myself and give my all to my education. But the school was every bit as disordered as I'd imagined it would be.

My attempts to learn were laughed at by other students. Early on, I might have raised my hand to ask a question or two, but the fallout—snickering, rude comments, being called names like pizza face due to a new severe acne flare-up—had a chilling effect on my psyche. No matter how hard I tried, I just didn't fit in. After a while, it was simply easier to join the crowd, even if I knew the crowd was someday headed collectively off a cliff. I desperately needed to belong somewhere and to be accepted by someone, anyone really.

I quickly figured out it was easier still to skip school altogether, which I began to do full-bore. At one point, I'd ditched school 40 days in a row. Forty days straight and not even a visit by the truant officer. *That* wouldn't have happened at the Catholic school, and I knew this. I was lost and spiraling badly, which I also knew.

There was one social studies teacher who took an interest in me, a white guy who was probably in his early

30s. He approached me with an attendance book and an ultimatum.

"Listen, you've got a choice," he said rather curtly. "You're either going to meet me before school starts each morning to get some tutoring so you can catch up, or I'm going to call your mother and tell her you're not coming to school."

I thought about it for only a second. I chose the former and said I'd come early the next day. He smiled and nodded.

"Be here tomorrow at 6:30 in the morning," he instructed me.

"But school doesn't start until 7:45," I countered.

"Well, I've got lots of tutoring to do. You're severely behind," he said. "See you then."

He tutored me all right. But never about social studies. We'd meet in an empty classroom when it was still dark outside. No students and hardly any teachers were in the building. He'd always begin under the auspices of some lesson plan with "We're going to study the _____ today." After a few minutes, he was only studying me.

At first, it was come-ons poorly disguised as compliments. Then, it was light touches, the brush of his knees across mine as we sat at desks facing each other. Hugs goodbye when the first period bell rang became hugs hello the next morning. Then kisses. Then squeezes and inappropriate feels.

During our sessions, I never learned much about the Great Depression or anything else, for that matter. But I certainly fell into a depression much deeper than the one I'd already lived in, if that's even possible. Apparently, it was.

I'd been trapped by a social studies teacher. I felt like I'd fallen into a well, where even if I'd screamed at the top of my lungs, it would only echo within the walls. Nobody would hear me in the darkness. Nobody would believe me. I'd skipped enough school that he could fail me if he chose to. If I didn't show up for our early morning so-called tutoring sessions, I knew he'd call my mom or, worse, have me expelled and transferred to an even shoddier school.

I continued to begin my school days with his advances, sometimes fending them off, other times unable to, and always praying for the bell to ring.

I wanted to die. I don't mean that as a figure of speech. I wanted to *die*.

My grades were garbage, and my future was fading and bleak. My social studies teacher loomed large every morning, and I couldn't see a way out.

I'd gotten my hands on some pills. I'd swiped a few from God knows where. I didn't know what kind of pills they were, but I thought if I took a pill cocktail—swallow a heaping handful, all in one gulp—at least some of them would do their thing enough to kill me.

I told my older play sister about my plan. She was spending the night with me, so she would likely be the one who'd find my cold body in the morning.

"Listen, I'm taking a handful of pills tonight," I told her.

"Okay," she said. I hadn't expected much more of a response from her. We were close for a reason. Bonded by trauma. She was going through a terrible time with her mom, and her emotions were numbed out, just like mine.

"I'm going to swallow them all and lie down and slowly die," I reiterated for clarity.

"Okay," she said.

"If I'm dead in the morning, just tell my mom you don't know what happened."

"Okay."

"But if I'm in a coma, you'll probably need to call 911."

"Okay."

"So here goes," I said. With that, I popped a dozen or so different colored and shaped pills into my mouth like other kids do M&Ms, chased them with a half-glass of tap water, and lay down on my bed to meet my maker. "Tell Grammy I love her."

"Okay."

And that was that. My best friend rolled over and went to sleep while I lay on my back in the dark, waiting for the light.

My alarm went off at exactly six o'clock the next morning. I shouldn't have heard it, being dead and all, but I did. I instinctively swatted at the clock and silenced it.

I had a splitting headache, a massive one. But that was it. I was alive and in my room. My friend, still sleeping, wouldn't have to explain my death to Mom or call an ambulance after all.

For whatever reason, God did not let me die. Even though I'd learned to hate my life and even myself by then, He kept me around for more. At the time, it was something I could never fully understand.

I sat up and changed into my school clothes. After grabbing a quick bite to eat, I headed once again for my social studies tutoring session.

Everybody remembers their first job. Mine was at Burger King.

I loved working at BK. Taking orders, sneaking fries. For the first time in my life, I was making money. My money. I didn't have to ask Mom, Dad, or Grammy for a few bucks anymore. Every two weeks, a paycheck appeared with my name on it. My name. With cash in my checking account, I felt like a King myself. I could buy my own clothes. I could go to the mall and shop. I could also pay for my own food or drinks or movies, and even pick up groceries for our house when Mom was a little light.

My job empowered me. It gave me a sense of control. I began to climb the Burger King ladder, working longer hours and taking on bigger responsibilities.

On-the-job romance isn't an uncommon occurrence. It happens to a lot of people. In my case, his name was J.

J was the first boy I ever loved. He was a couple of years older than me and easy to talk to. He really liked me, too. Our flirting during our shifts led to doing things together outside of BK, which led to us becoming inseparable.

At one point, J said he wanted to marry me one day, and he was very intentional about that.

Young love doesn't go unnoticed, and my friends, including the girl who'd watched me try to OD and said only "Okay" a few months earlier, were jealous of my relationship with J because he was the real deal. A genuine, well-mannered, straight-laced, good student and a good young man to his core, with a bright future ahead.

They said things like he was too old for me, that he'd only use me and move on. They said I was missing out on good partying by spending all of my free time with him. They said it wouldn't end well, that I'd be dogged and dropped, and he'd break my heart, that I was only a freshman and deserved to play the field.

At some point, I began to believe them. They spoke the ever-familiar language of unworthiness, which I SO identified with. Surely, a girl like me couldn't really make it last with a stand-up guy like J. I soon began to search for fault lines with J, little, tiny cracks I could pry apart.

J's mother was an alcoholic, so he didn't drink and had a strict policy on staying away from it and all other bad things. He was so good to me. His goodness should have set me free, but instead, it became an albatross around my neck: heavy, haunting, and undeserved. It was a constant reminder of everything I wasn't, and something I felt I could never live up to. I began to accuse him of not being fun, which wasn't even slightly true. If he tried to get closer to me, which he often did, I'd begin to push him away. But J was a nice guy, always forgiving, always taking me back without questions or grudges. He showed me way more love than I could even muster for myself or receive.

In my sophomore year, J asked me to his senior prom. It was an elegant affair. He was dressed in his rented tux, and I in my fancy blush-pink gown. There were photos at my house and a corsage on my wrist. He'd methodically set aside a portion of his Burger King paychecks to save up for a real dinner for us afterward. J was a true gentleman. He was a one-of-a-kind, once-in-a-lifetime kind of guy.

But I'd been poisoned and was ready to go in for the kill. Self-sabotage was my new drug of choice. That prom night, which should have been a seminal moment in our young lives, was ruined, along with our relationship, by my actions and my actions alone. I treated him terribly that evening. I was absolutely dreadful.

That prom night, I broke it off with J for good. I didn't give him a reason because I didn't have one. I remember saying, "I'm done. I don't want to do this anymore."

Ever the gentleman, he tried to reason with me, salvage prom night, and save our relationship. He even tried to save our friendship. But I would have none of it. The deep shame and unworthiness I carried were much stronger, and he never even knew what hit him.

I ended the night alone, wearing a crumpled prom gown and a wilting flower. Although he came to my home several times, pleading with me to talk things out to restore our relationship and future, I went radio silent. At some point, J realized my mind, crazy as it was, was nevertheless made up. He graciously exited the stage that was my life. He wished me well, kissed my forehead, and gracefully bowed out.

A few weeks later, immediately following his high school graduation, J left Burger King for Uncle Sam. He'd enlisted in the U.S. Navy and, without a word, departed from my world forever.

Someone at BK broke the news to me that his recruiters actually arrived at his graduation and took him away for boot camp immediately afterward. I never saw J again.

With J gone for good, things didn't take long to spiral completely out of control. The depression returned, and more peer pressure led to more drinking, smoking weed, and ingesting any kind of drug that could numb me to reality. High school still sucked, and my home life wasn't much better. If I didn't want to necessarily die any longer, I, at least, wanted to live to get high.

I was 16 years old when I met Sherman.

He was cute, and he liked to party. My kind of man. We'd often take off to the Westside of Chicago and the Lakefront, where we'd meet up with other friends. Or we'd invite ourselves to someone's apartment and do our thing. We'd get drunk and stoned and have sex. It became a fun routine.

With time, Sherman's drug use got heavier. And because he was my guy, my drug use did, too. Weed begat coke. Coke begat heroin. If Sherman showed up with pills to snort, shrooms, wiki, or whatever, I was first in line. I only drew the line at shooting up, as if that was a moral standard.

We'd get wasted together and prepare elaborate meals like steaks, crab legs, and clam chowder. We laughed and danced and woke the neighbors. We'd fall into hours-long dope nods, and we'd sleep into the afternoon following all-night parties.

I wasn't quite aware of this at the time, but Sherman was a functional junkie and an intelligent one. He was in college studying engineering and wanted to be an electrical engineer. He was also well-versed in architecture and building styles, everything from classic Greek or Roman to Modern Contemporary. He opened my mind and world to engineering, architecture, and psychology.

We'd snort heroin and go driving around Chicago. Sherman talked the whole time, pointing out the different architectural styles. Sitting next to him, I was mesmerized by his depth of knowledge. There's nothing sexier than an intellectual mind, even if it's baked most of the time.

I'd dropped out of high school halfway through my junior year, becoming another statistic but not caring a whit. I'd half-heartedly tried to get my GED by enrolling in night school, but my partying took precedence, so I quit that, too. By this point in my life, I'd simply given up and given in to the voices of everyone who constantly said I'd never be or do anything with my life. I had nothing to attain, and I was pretty hopeless.

By my 18th birthday, I'd left Burger King and was working full-time at Zayre, a chain of then-popular discount stores.

Zayre paid better than BK, and the work was pretty easy, but I hated dealing with the public, so I quit there, too. I signed up with a temp agency that placed me in low-level administrative office jobs, keeping a paycheck coming in and keeping us partying constantly.

And then my entire world changed when I got pregnant with Brittani.

To his credit, Sherman asked me to marry him. We had a quick little ceremony at my childhood church on July 22, 1989, when I was four months pregnant and barely showing.

Suddenly, my mind and thoughts about everything changed. I stopped drinking and had no desire for drugs or partying anymore. Being married and now pregnant again was the greatest joy I'd ever experienced. Being a wife and a mom were the extreme desires of my heart. Desires that I had as early as second grade. Desires I never shared with anyone but God, whom I spoke to from time to time.

But fulfilling a dream and knowing how to handle it are vastly different things. Sherman and I rented our first apartment in Forest Park, Illinois. It was a nicer area in the suburbs, and the apartment was nice too. I felt very blessed to have our own place, to both be gainfully employed and to be able to take care of ourselves at such a young age.

Sherman was very tender and gentle with me while I was pregnant. He cared for me in a way that was so sweet and very foreign to me, and I loved it to my core. I found joy in coming home from work every day, cooking a nice meal, and maintaining our new place. And probably for the very first time in my life, I was experiencing what I thought to be bliss.

CHAPTER 6

# DON'T KILL SHERMAN

*"There are moments in life that can shatter*
*the very ground beneath you—when everything you*
*thought you knew falls apart. In that silence,*
*a single question rises: Where do I go from here?"*

—Tami Franklin

I had a relatively easy and uneventful pregnancy. I loved everything about being pregnant—pregnancy glow and all. I was
placed on bed rest toward the end of my pregnancy due to pre-
eclampsia. My blood pressure was high, and my legs and ankles
were swollen with a shining belly about to burst.

Sherman would drop me off at Grammy's home every weekday morning on his way to work. I'd hang out with her, talking
and laughing, connecting, bonding, watching TV together, and,
of course, eating her home cooking. Pregnant women love to
eat, and Grammy was still the best cook on planet Earth. It was
just like old times with us.

On the weekends, I'd stay at home, almost always by myself.
Sherman was off work on Saturdays and Sundays but was

seldom around our apartment. He'd go out with his friends. He would party and come back late.

I was in the ninth month of pregnancy, expecting a little girl who'd be named Brittani Chantal. It was early December, the start of the much-anticipated Christmas season. I'd arrived at my due date of December 4, 1989, so Brittani could check in at any minute.

I was content enough, though, doing my best to make our place a comfortable, loving home. I enjoyed decorating for Christmas and wrapping Brittani's first presents from Santa. I was so excited. I sat and waited for my water to break. It was the first time in my life that I felt the joy of the holidays and the thought of having my own little family soon. The dream I had since I was a little girl of being a wife and a mom was now becoming a reality. I recalled how often I used to daydream about this time in my life, and it brought a beautiful smile to my heart. That was until I heard Sherman's footsteps approaching.

It was December 6, around two o'clock in the morning. I was in bed when I heard Sherman's footsteps coming down the hallway. I could always tell his state of mind by his footsteps. He was walking faster and louder than usual that night. Almost running, I could tell, his 6'3" gait causing a racket.

He opened the front door loudly, out of breath. I could hear him panting. From our bed, I heard him fling open the kitchen cabinets and begin wildly throwing pots and pans onto the kitchen floor. If our neighbors weren't up already, they were up now.

*What the ... ?* I thought. I got out of bed, a bit groggy, and walked into the kitchen.

His eyes met mine. He looked panicked and terrified. He continued to clear out the cabinets noisily.

"Sherman, what are you *doing?*" I asked. "What's going on?"

"I just killed someone," he said.

The sentence took a beat or two to register in my mind.

"You did *what?*" I said, still not comprehending what I'd just heard.

He hurried to the living room window that looked out onto the street below.

"You did what?!" I screamed. "What do you mean you killed someone?!"

"I killed someone," he said, looking directly into my eyes. I could see he meant it.

"I think I see police cars," he said, throwing the curtain back.

He ran to the kitchen, tripped over a frying pan, crawled headfirst into the lower kitchen cabinets, and folded his lanky frame into a ball to fit.

"Just keep looking out the window," he said. "Let me know when they're gone." With those instructions, he closed the cabinet door from the inside.

Sure enough, a police car was outside. I watched it stop, and two officers got out. I provided Sherman with a surreal play-by-play, keeping one eye on the cops while wondering where I should put the pots and pans if they headed our way.

From the window, I saw the policemen knock on an apartment door across the complex's commons area. They knocked loudly again. A light came on inside the apartment, somebody answered the door, and the cops began talking with them. I could tell from their mannerisms that they'd found the person they were looking for. Their conversation lasted only a couple of minutes. The cops returned to their car and drove away. They weren't looking for Sherman after all. It was an unbelievable coincidence.

I told him it was okay for him to leave the kitchen cabinets. He crawled out and stood up.

I collapsed onto the floor, sobbing on my hands and knees, my nine-month-pregnant body convulsing in panic, in fear, in utter confusion like I'd never known before. I just went from thinking about Christmas to thinking about murder. I cried and wept throughout the night in fear, with a million thoughts and feelings running through my mind and body.

I could tell my grief affected my baby, too, because she was suddenly very still. She felt like a hard log inside me, shocked by the trauma of grief she was feeling from me. I recall having to physically make myself stop sobbing so my baby would have a fighting chance.

In the morning, after he'd come off his high, Sherman told me what had happened. He'd gone to Keith's house. Keith and his brother, whom I'd grown up with back in my old neighborhood, were big-time drug dealers. Sherman had become friendly with Keith by buying drugs, so he allowed Sherman to come to his house to make his purchases, which he had done the night before.

Only this time, when Sherman got to the house, Keith wasn't there.

Keith's girlfriend was alone in the house with her two boys, ages one and two. She let Sherman in.

Sherman told me he knew where Keith's safe was located, in a back room away from the street. He knew Keith kept an ample supply of drugs and money in it. He knew the only thing between him and the safe was a petite female and her two tiny boys.

Sherman said he jumped on the mother and, while her sons watched, strangled her to death. He then grabbed the safe and turned to run back toward the front door, hearing the little boys crying as he ran past them.

But as Sherman crossed the living room, someone, probably Keith, was coming through the very same door. Sherman dropped the safe, turned, and ran back through the apartment and out the back door. He ran down an alley and jumped into my car, the one he'd taken that night, but he was too nervous to start it. He bailed, leaving it there, and ran away into the night.

Sherman then called his mother and made up an excuse that he was hanging out with his boys and didn't want to drive home after a night of drinking, partying, etc. This was not an uncommon occurrence, so his mom didn't hesitate to come and get him, and he had her drop him off at our apartment.

"I think he saw my jacket," Sherman said.

I didn't understand. I was in complete and utter shock.

Sherman explained that if Keith had seen the color of his jacket, it would be enough to possibly identify him for the murder. He said he had to get rid of the jacket. He was adamant about it. He said he had to concoct an alibi regarding where he was that night.

He said he was going to call his mom.

"Call your mom?" I asked incredulously.

"Yes," he said.

He knew his mom would help him. He dialed her number. He told his mother the whole story—how he'd gone there to buy drugs, how he'd strangled to death Keith's girlfriend in front of her two boys, how he'd stolen the safe and dropped it when someone came through the front door, how he'd run away.

Sure enough, his mom offered to help him get rid of the jacket. I was astounded!

In little time, she arrived at our apartment complex, picked us up out front, and drove to Chicago's West Side to dump the jacket in a random alley dumpster, all the while fabricating a detailed fake itinerary of what had happened the night before, where Sherman allegedly was, and with whom.

I desperately wanted to stay home, but Sherman wouldn't allow me to stay behind for fear I would call the police or flee the apartment. He also said he wanted his pregnant wife with him at all times as some sort of insurance policy in case the police were on the hunt for him. Ensuring his own safety, not mine or our unborn baby's.

In the car, there was never any talk about the dead young mother on the floor—no concern about her two little boys. There was certainly no intention of calling the police or doing what was right, which was even more chilling to me.

A few days later, my mom called me, upset with bad news.

"Oh my God, Tami, I've got to tell you. This young girl from Maywood was killed the other night. Somebody strangled her to death for no reason," my mom said.

I was silent.

"She had two little boys. They were there when she was killed. She was so popular; everyone knew her. It's just so senseless and sad," Mom said.

I said nothing.

"I'm going to the funeral on Saturday. You might want to come, Tami," she said.

I didn't go to the funeral. It would have been an audacious thing to do. But I was at my mother's apartment that Saturday afternoon when she returned from it. She just shook her head as she walked into the living room, muttering something about how pointless and tragic it all seemed.

As my mother passed me, she dropped into my lap a small, folded obituary she'd picked up when signing the guestbook at the funeral home. A picture of a vibrant, smiling, beautiful young woman was on the front of it. Inside was her obituary. As I laid the obituary down on the table, I saw the *Chicago Tribune* lying there. And on the front page, in bold letters, "POLICE SUSPECT DRUG LINK IN SLAYING."

"What kind of person could do such a thing?" she said to herself as she walked into her bedroom to change clothes.

I knew exactly the kind of person who could do such a thing. My husband. The father of my soon-to-be-born child. Sherman could do such a thing. Sherman did such a thing.

I rubbed my belly, felt Brittani kick, and said nothing. I was numb. So was she … already impacted by the world outside of the womb.

Four days later, I was still numb, in shock, and afraid to even think about what I knew when it was time for my weekly doctor's appointment, a status checkup on my pregnancy. Brittani was due to arrive any day. By this time, my vision had gotten blurry, my blood pressure was still rather high, and my ankles were swollen to twice their normal size.

"We're going to induce you later today," the doctor said matter-of-factly.

I was ready for the pregnancy to be over, ready to meet my baby girl, but the shock of hearing the word "induce" meant her arrival was imminent.

"Go home and get your things," he said. "Get your husband and meet me at the hospital."

I followed his instructions and, two hours later, checked into the hospital. They wheelchaired me to a room, stuck me with the proper IVs and monitoring devices, and began induction.

If inducing someone sounds like it's quickening the delivery process, speeding things up, that's what I thought, too. It's not necessarily that, or at least not in my case. I went into labor all right, but the labor lasted 30 hours. A full day-plus of contractions getting closer and closer, of excruciating pain most women will say is unlike anything they've ever felt.

Sherman was in a dope nod a majority of the time.

He was asleep in a chair beside my hospital bed. As nurses, attendants, and physician assistants came and went, as the beeping sounds of a half dozen medical monitoring devices littered the air, my husband, high as usual, slept.

He'd wake up occasionally, glance around the room, and pass out again. He'd insisted on bringing an oil painting he was working on, a hobby he said he'd taken up to pass the time and keep his thoughts at bay, but little painting got done in that room.

I moaned in birth pains while my husband deadened his reality.

As I lay there, waiting for Brittani to appear, I thought about the current state of my life.

My mom and I weren't ever really close. When I married Sherman and moved into our own place, she went to stay with a family member.

Unfortunately, I was never too close to my brother. When he showed natural talent as a pianist, a child prodigy who played by ear, Mom seemed to shower him with attention and what felt like favoritism. This only widened the gulf between Tim and me for a time.

I loved my Grammy dearly, and she loved me unconditionally. But I didn't dare bring her any closer into my life, knowing my husband was a murderer. I knew by now what Sherman was capable of doing, what he had indeed done. To confide my problems to my grandmother might be a death sentence for us both. No, Grammy needed to be protected by me. I owed her that much.

If I'd told my dad anything, he might've quite literally killed Sherman, for all I know. Dad was a very calm, laid-back, gentle man, but I can only imagine what this information would do to him. To protect me and his new grandbaby, my dad would have likely confronted my husband, and the result would not have been pretty. I'd grown even closer to my dad in recent years, and I knew he loved me dearly. He loved Brittani dearly, too, even though she was still a few hours away from being born. No, I couldn't tell him, either.

And that was everyone. I had no close friends. There were no more teachers and no mentors. My circle was small, and I was isolated in an unhealthy way.

At that moment, I could count on less than one hand the people who I thought could offer me protection, who could help out my baby and me if we needed it. But I wouldn't enlist those few people I was sure would help us, Grammy and Dad, for fear of what it would trigger in Sherman or them.

So, I sat there in a darkened hospital room and waited for my baby to be born, watching my husband nodding from his dope high, wondering what my life had become.

"The baby is under stress, and we're going to do a C-section," said the doctor, who'd burst into the room, his decision already made.

His words startled me back to the present.

In short order, the room brightened and filled with people in all different shades of medical garb. My legs were placed in stirrups as the attendants gathered around, and after the final flurry of preparation, my baby girl entered the world.

I'd like to think Sherman was relatively sober when his daughter was born, but I can't guarantee it. He was, nevertheless, a happy man.

"Here's my baby girl," I remember him saying when a nurse handed Brittani to him for the first time. "My little baby girl."

He was beaming with joy while holding a life he'd helped create.

For four months, Brittani, Sherman, and I lived an existence that seemed like a fairy tale. We doted on her and made detailed notes of her every little accomplishment. Her first bath. The first time she raised her head on her own. Every giggle and poop.

We took hundreds of pictures. We laughed hundreds of times. We'd lie there in bed, the three of us, Mommy and Daddy staring in wonder at our tiny miracle.

I'd never been so strangely happy in all my life. Dissociation was now my drug of choice. It was easy and felt like a safe place.

Brittani immediately improved my life! Her presence saved my soul. I felt more alive than ever before, more thankful for the world around me. I prayed to Jesus that she had changed Sherman's life, too.

But with every knock on the door, I'd panic, wondering who was on the other side and why. With every siren wailing in the street outside, my stomach would sink and bring me back to the reality that my husband, Brittani's dad, was a cold-hearted killer. I constantly feared it wouldn't be long until some detective connected the dots that led to Sherman.

Sometimes, I felt guilty rocking my baby to sleep when I knew there were two little boys in Maywood who would never be rocked by their mother again. I tried not to think about it. I tried hard to wish the trauma of it all away, but the feeling always returned, reminding me that neither a killer nor the truth can hide in the kitchen cabinets forever.

"Sleep, little Brittani, sleep," I said as I kissed her perfect little head. "Mommy's here."

# CHAPTER 7

# TEDDY BEAR

*"Everything that happens to you is your teacher.*
*The secret is to learn to sit at the feet of your own life*
*and be taught by it."*

–Polly B. Brends

With Brittani home and both mine and Sherman's steady work paying the bills, in my mind's eye, I could see the next 40 years of my life unfold. Sherman and I would buy a house in the suburbs and raise our baby together, grow old in the comfort of each other, and retire to some beach community, sipping iced tea and watching sunsets.

Only that vision was as temporary as an afternoon beer buzz. Before long, the abuse started.

I'd quit drugs and alcohol when I learned I was pregnant. Sherman had not. Sherman was extremely tender with me and very attentive throughout my entire pregnancy, but that was a very different reality once I'd given birth.

Not only was he still using, but his choice of drug had also migrated exclusively to heroin. Sherman had dropped out of

college a few credits shy of an associate's degree to take a job at
a scientific laboratory. With two paychecks coming in, we were
getting by pretty well for our age. We had a rented apartment.
We'd bought a car and some furniture. We were raising Brittani
while we were still practically children ourselves, ages 18 and
21. We were limping along.

But heroin's grip is viselike. It takes over a person's soul and
corrupts it to the core. That same cute, smart, conversational
guy I'd fallen for a couple of years earlier was becoming another
creature altogether, an unpredictable and violent one at that.

At first, Sherman berated me for no reason. He'd look for
and find fault in something I'd done and fly into a sustained rage,
screaming, pushing, and jumping on me without provocation.

From there, it got even darker. I'd fall asleep after a tough
day at work or after taking care of Brittani, and awake screaming in pain as he'd snuff out his cigarette in my hand or on my
arm or punch my face repeatedly. I've still got the physical scars
from this season in my life. His volatility toward me was sudden
and terrifying. He'd be decent and calm as long as he'd gotten
his fix, but when the drug wore off, he was a different animal, a
wild and dangerous one.

Sherman would threaten my life often. He'd punch holes
in our apartment walls. He'd even go on benders that would
keep him away from home for hours, returning only to demand
money and then leaving again. On an afternoon family drive
one day, with Brittani in her baby seat and me riding shotgun,
he shattered our car's windshield with his fist without a prompt
or warning.

Understandably, I'd grown deathly afraid of Sherman. I was
afraid for Brittani, although he never touched her in a harmful
way, but I was afraid for our well-being. It was like living within

a powder keg, never knowing when he'd return enraged and strike a match.

I retreated into the fear. Positive, loving relationships I'd once enjoyed with my Grammy and Dad became strained. I'd grown even more distant from my mom. Sherman succeeded in putting up a wall between me and whoever else I'd loved before him. I'd become a means to his drug-addled end, someone to hit up for cash to keep the beast of withdrawal at bay.

I believed that the postcard life I'd once imagined would never come to pass. I'd become a prisoner within the home I'd tried so hard to create. I'd come to the sobering realization that I was married to a psychopath. My husband and the father of my baby was a dangerous junkie. I was 19 years old and didn't know what to do.

On nights when he was away somewhere, which was often, I'd rock Brittani to sleep while praying to Jesus to help change things. In those rare moments of peace, when it was just me and my baby and God, I'd think about a lot of things. I'd think about how much I missed Jeannine and wonder what Grammy was doing. I'd think about drinking black coffee with Dad, eating government cheese, or beating the neighborhood boys in foot races. I'd wonder what J was up to—all of which seemed like a lifetime ago. I'd fall asleep holding my baby, and all was right with the world in those sacred moments.

While those first four months of Brittani's life had been among the most joyous of mine, the time we shared doting on our precious new daughter soon turned into something entirely different.

I went back to work after four months' maternity leave, and things headed south quickly. With me away each day, Sherman's drug abuse escalated. He denied it at first, but I knew him well. I could tell by his mood swings, his paranoid thoughts, his sudden departures at all hours for God-knows-where, and the phone calls to and from seedy people at all hours as they spoke in some abbreviated drug code. And I'd find evidence, usually in the car, of his use, including syringes, discarded needles, and empty plastic bags.

I worried about the possibility of Sherman catching AIDS from a shared needle. I worried about him giving it to me.

Even when we were together as a family, life was unpredictable. One day, we were out for a family drive in Chicago. Sherman was behind the wheel. Brittani and I were in our usual spots in the car. I was chatting away about nothing in particular when I heard, "Hold on just a minute."

Sherman screeched the car to a sudden halt right in the middle of a city street, reached onto the backseat floor for a baseball bat, flung open his door, and hurried to the nearby sidewalk. I was still trying to figure out what was going on, when suddenly—CLUNK.

He'd swung the bat like Sammy Sosa and connected upside some unsuspecting passerby's head. He'd knocked him out cold. The guy lay there on a busy street on the West Side, unconscious, perhaps dead. Sherman walked back to the car, put the bat back onto the floor behind him, and zoomed off.

"What da' hell?" I said.

"That dude owed me money," he said.

And that was that. He said no more. I knew if I were to press the issue, he might very well take batting practice on me, too. We continued on our afternoon family drive. We were certainly *not* the Huxtables.

Scenes like this became increasingly more common and more volatile with each passing day. As Sherman sank deeper into addiction, any semblance of normalcy evaporated. He soon lost his job, so money became an issue. Bills were due, and food in the fridge became scarce. Any income I made went out and into my husband's veins. I knew I needed to get out of the marriage, but I didn't know how. If I pressed it, my husband was liable to kill me.

I was taking Brittani to daycare one weekday morning when Sherman asked to ride along. A rather odd request, yes, but I assumed he needed a lift to find a fix. I'd taken the baby into the center, said my goodbyes to her, and returned to the car, pulling back onto the road and toward my office.

"You're not going to work today," he said sternly. "You're going to call in sick."

I looked at him in confusion.

"Your dad gave you some money," he said.

My blood ran cold. My dad had indeed given me money for savings a few months before. He'd worked hard and saved to gift me a good amount of money. My dad was so proud, so happy to put that money in my hand; I teared up when he did. It was a cushion for life's rainy days, he said.

"You're going to go to the bank and get that money," Sherman said. "And you're going to give that money to me."

My heart sank. I felt like vomiting. But I knew what my husband was capable of, anything really, so I said not a word and drove on.

"Listen to me. When we get to that bank, if you alert anybody—some teller, some security guard, if you do *anything* that tells them I'm forcing you to take this money out—I'll kill you. Do you understand me?"

I nodded slightly.

"I'll kill you, and I'll kill everyone in that bank," he said for good measure.

He showed me a gun.

I pulled into the bank's parking lot. Sherman followed me closely inside.

As I passed a security guard on his stool by the door, I made eye contact with him. I tried to give the guard my best "please help me" look, trying to make my eyes talk. "Save me," they screamed. But the security guard didn't notice. He smiled hello, and onward I walked with Sherman right behind me.

At the teller's window, I provided my ID and told her I wanted to withdraw all the money in my account. With the teller, I tried again to project a look of fear, of being coerced. She didn't get it, either, and matter-of-factly went about processing my request.

For a split second, it crossed my mind to scream out. But all I could envision was a bloodbath inside the lobby, first me being shot in the head, and then everyone else. Perhaps the security guard would leap into action, or perhaps he wouldn't. Either way, if I screamed, I died. I knew that much.

The teller returned and began counting out the money like tellers do. I stared at the counter in front of me as hundred-dollar bills and then twenties were doled out into a neat pile. She selected a white envelope with the bank's logo from a drawer, put the money inside, and handed it to me.

"Will there be anything else today?" she asked.

I took the envelope from her hand and slowly shook my head no.

"Well, thank you, and have a nice day," she said cheerily.

I didn't respond. I turned around, walked back across the lobby, and tried, in a last-ditch effort, to telepathically cry,

"Please help me" as I passed the security guard, but he, too, said, "Have a nice day."

Inside the car, Sherman told me to give him the envelope. He told me to drive home, and, when we arrived, he told me to get out. He took the car and drove away.

Inside our apartment, I sat numb for hours, unsure of what to do. My dad had worked overtime for that money. He'd scrimped and saved, little by little, and undoubtedly kept it hidden away. The thought of that made me cry. I remembered how thrilled I was when my Dad had given it to me, how I swelled inside with joy. I thought maybe someday we'd use a little bit of it for a nice family vacation, maybe to Disney World or somewhere fun. I'd thought it could be a down payment on a house for the three of us or maybe the makings of a college fund for Brittani. At the very least, it was a security blanket of sorts, a guard against unemployment or an unforeseen medical expense. Now, it was in Sherman's hands and probably not for very long.

I was still deep in thought when the phone rang. I answered reluctantly.

The voice on the other end asked for me. "Speaking," I said.

The voice identified himself as a sheriff's deputy. He said my car had been found crashed on the freeway headed toward the West Side of Chicago. There was nobody inside it when the police arrived. It had been abandoned alongside the road.

"Were you driving the car?" the deputy asked.

"No," I responded. "I'm here at home."

"Who was driving your car, ma'am?" he asked.

"My husband had the car," I heard myself say.

"You need to come down to the station," the policeman replied. "We're going to need to talk with you."

I agreed, hung up, and tried to conceive what might have happened and how I would get to the sheriff's department when the apartment door burst open. It was Sherman.

"I wrecked the car and left it on the side of the 290 Expressway," he said. "You've got to tell the sheriff you were driving. You can't say I was driving. You were the one driving, understand?!"

I sat motionless on the sofa. Silent, scared, and aware that my world was crashing down around me.

"Understand? *Do you understand me!?*" my husband screamed.

I nodded, "Yes."

When my dad found out about the car, he bought me a new one—well, a new used one—something that would get me to work and back. A reliable vehicle for getting around. That's what dads do.

By now, I was beginning to plot my escape plan. I knew I couldn't stay with Sherman much longer. His drug use was at a fever pitch. The threats of violence against me were increasing. The atmosphere when he was present was always volatile. I didn't want to raise Brittani in a world ripe with drugs and violence and so many unknowns, especially with someone capable of murder.

One day, I decided to make the move. Sherman had been out for days on a binge, I presumed, when I decided to change the locks on our apartment door. I'd gotten a handyman to do it and, when the job was finished, settled inside what suddenly felt like a vault. I relaxed on the sofa while I ran different escape scenarios through my head.

I kept wondering: *When would I do it? Where would I go? How would he react?*

I'd fallen asleep when I was awakened by Sherman's voice coming through the apartment door. I heard him thank the apartment manager, who had a spare of the new key, for letting him inside, saying how silly he was for forgetting his keys on his dresser and how it wouldn't happen again.

He closed the door behind him and stood towering over me as I lay terrified on the sofa.

He lunged at me and put his hand over my mouth as a struggle ensued. From the hallway, I heard the apartment manager say, "Hey, everything okay in there?"

Sherman whispered into my ear, "If you say anything, I'll kill you. Tell him everything's okay."

"Everything's okay," I said, trying to sound normal.

Sherman waited a few seconds until the manager's footsteps trailed off. He beat me to a bloody pulp, then strangled me until I nearly lost consciousness. It was the worst he'd ever beaten me.

"How *dare* you lock me out of my place."

"This is *my* place."

"I'm *never* leaving, you got *that*?"

With every sentence came another blow. With his fists. With his feet. With his fists again.

"Where's Brittani?" he screamed, looking around the apartment. "I'm taking Brittani."

He was out-of-his-mind high, didn't know what day it was, nor the fact that his daughter was at daycare.

"*No*, you're *not* getting her," I screamed at him, for which I received another few punches and kicks that knocked me into and over the water cooler.

"Where is she?!" he demanded, growing increasingly more agitated.

He turned, hit me again as I lay curled in a shivering, horrified ball on the floor, and stormed away, slamming the apartment door behind him and yelling I'd better remember whose apartment it was.

I called my mom to come get me. I was badly beaten, bleeding everywhere, but it was time to pick up my daughter. On the drive to the daycare center, I tried to calm down and put myself back together, at least enough to make a quick appearance to get my baby. It was finally time for what many people call a *Come-to-Jesus* talk.

"Tami, I haven't said anything until now," Mom began. I listened, not saying a word.

"Listen to me," she continued, addressing me sternly but with sober concern. "You are in danger. Brittani is in danger. Don't you know you deserve better than this?! You have got to wake up and smell the coffee. You've *got* to get *away* from him. You've got to *do* something."

I promised my mom I would get away from Sherman for good. I told her I'd changed the locks, the very act that had set him off.

"You've got to do something, Tami," I heard her say again as I walked across the sidewalk into the daycare center.

One of the center's attendants smiled and greeted me, but her expression quickly shifted to shock when she saw my face. I didn't give her a chance to ask what happened. I glanced around the room for Brittani, but I didn't see her. Then I heard the most dreaded news.

"Your husband picked her up a little while ago," she said.

I turned and ran outside, back to my mom. He'd taken my baby to God-knows-where, where he was doing God-knows-what with God-knows-who. She was a six-month-old baby, helpless, and he was wasted and out of control.

Mom was right; I *had* to do something.

For some reason, I didn't believe Sherman had kidnapped Brittani, and I knew he wouldn't harm her. In all the ways he'd beat and abuse me, Brittani was his true heart; he was always good to her. He cherished her, and she loved her dad. I guess, knowing him like I did, I figured he simply wanted to see her and took her along for a joyride as he bought heroin and shot up even more. I could see him showing her off to his drug friends, acting like he was Father of the Year. He'd bounce her on his knee, and they'd laugh. The novelty would pass, though; it always does, and he'd eventually want to get rid of the baby and head somewhere else to party.

I told my mom to take me home. Once there, I sat and waited, knowing Sherman would return with Brittani.

A few hours later, long after dark, Sherman returned carrying our baby, asleep in his arms. He walked through the unlocked apartment door. Without saying a word, I watched him put her gently into bed, kiss her forehead, and whisper goodnight. For a moment, it all seemed so normal. In that instance, my life felt so beautifully, wonderfully, peacefully normal.

Then Sherman turned into a rage-filled demon and violently raped and sodomized me. After he fell asleep, I lay on the floor, silent tears rolling down my face. I knew tomorrow had to be the day I would escape at all costs!

The next day, Brittani and I finally escaped and moved in with Grammy. I knew in the fold of my family and neighborhood, I would be safe. Fear and isolation previously made me believe the opposite truth. But truthfully, I felt safer and more protected than I'd felt in a very long time. Grammy began watching Brittani by day. My mom drove me to work, and a co-worker drove me home every day. My relatives and friends from Maywood kept my spirits up.

Everyone was on the lookout for Sherman; lots of eyes around Maywood were watching out for me. I only wished I'd had the guts to leave Sherman sooner.

A few days later, while sitting at my desk inside the large corporate office of a Fortune 500 company, I looked up and saw Sherman walking directly toward me. He was being escorted by one of the executives, who happily pointed me out (not knowing the danger I was in). While they were still several yards away, I heard the manager say, "There's Tami right there."

"Let's go," Sherman said to me rather forcefully, without causing a scene.

I hesitated at first, feeling sickened, but I was painfully aware of the threats he'd made at the bank only a short time earlier. I assumed he'd still kill me and everyone else he could. I assumed he had his gun with him.

I followed him across the room and out of the building, leaving my purse behind. We got into an unfamiliar car and headed to the West Side. He said very little on the drive but made sure I had seen the gun.

We arrived outside what I presumed to be a dealer's place. Sherman disappeared inside and returned a few minutes later with a baggie of heroin. He turned the car around and headed to his father's house.

Sherman began to shoot up and tried desperately to get me to join him in getting high. It was like he felt that if we both did it, things would be okay between us. He'd ask me to join in, I'd refuse, and he'd shoot up some more. The cycle repeated itself several times until he began nodding off and then fell into a complete sleep.

I waited a while to make sure he was in a deep sleep before I took the car keys and left.

It was still early in the day, so I returned to work, believing if I'd simply make my abduction seem like a necessary departure—hey, my husband needed me for something—it would be no big deal. No such luck.

When I walked in, the company was swarming with police. When my coworkers saw me, there was a great commotion. My manager ran up to me.

"We believed you were kidnapped and taken against your will because you left your purse and all your personal effects behind, which seemed quite unusual for you," he said.

For the first time ever, I admitted out loud that it was indeed the case.

"Yes, I was kidnapped," I said. I felt complete relief for the first time in what seemed like a lifetime and said I was okay. I tried to return to my desk, but a cop intervened and asked me to come with him.

Inside the police car, I gave the officer my statement, telling him the whole story. It felt good to finally come clean. Maybe this is what Mom meant by, "You've got to do something."

I told the officer I was scared for my life if I didn't go with Sherman. I also told him about the gun he carries, about the smack he shoots, and about the threats and beatings. In that moment, I also told the truth about the rapes. The cop wrote it all down.

Ironically, I didn't divulge Sherman's ultimate crime to him. I'd been in so much turmoil and riddled with trauma that I'd literally forgotten about the one thing that would've earned him many years in jail, and Brit and I just as many years of peace and freedom.

As he put away his notebook, the policeman pulled out the previous day's *Chicago Sun-Times* newspaper. He handed it to me.

"I want you to look at this," he said.

On the front page was a photo of a young woman who'd been murdered by her husband. He told me to look closely and to read the article.

"You need to get away from your husband," he warned. "I don't want this to be you. I don't want to see your picture next in the *Sun-Times*."

He looked at me deeply, with honest, dad-like concern.

"I don't want to hear from you again," the cop said. "I like you and you seem like a nice young woman, but I don't want to hear from you again. I don't want to read this kind of story about you—ever! If you stay with him, though, I'm pretty sure I will."

I took a moment to let it sink in. Then, I thanked him for his concern.

"Do whatever you have to do to get out," he said. "Do *whatever* you have to do."

The next time I saw Sherman was at our divorce proceeding.

I was surrounded by security personnel that the judge had ordered. I was escorted into and out of the courthouse, and a police car followed me home. Within a few minutes that day, my husband became my ex-husband. He was ordered to stay far away from me.

After the hearing, though, he left his attorney's table and walked toward me. I could sense everyone's fear and heightened stress rise. The security guard stepped forward with his hand on his gun. My attorney even stepped in front of me to shield me, sensing danger. Sherman pulled something from a brown paper bag and pointed it toward me. I braced myself for shots to be fired when he said, "I got this teddy bear for Brittani. Just tell her I love her."

It was the last time I ever saw him.

# CHAPTER 8

# THE GIFT OF TIME

*"In life's most tumultuous seasons, time becomes a sacred gift—a gentle reminder that healing unfolds in moments, not milestones, and every second holds the power to restore, renew, and reveal purpose."*

—Tami Franklin

I've known instability and sexual, verbal, and physical abuse my entire life. I know what it feels like for your new husband to be a wanted man because he just killed somebody for drugs and a few dollars. But I never knew real fear until Brittani got sick.

The local media called it a "Super Surgery." It was a catchy headline, I must admit. We were interviewed by TV reporters. They often spoke with practiced amazement, an "oh my gosh, listen to this" cadence of reporting intended to keep viewers tuned in, while overly made-up anchors chatted about somebody else's nightmare before transitioning to the weather report.

It would be a 20-hour operation, nearly an entire day under anesthesia. The doctors would shut down Brittani's heart and put her on bypass. A lung machine would do the breathing for her. And bit by bit, Dr. Lieber would tediously pull and cut and yank and carve out the tumor that had wrapped itself around my baby's spine, knowing that any slip or mishap could render Brittani permanently paralyzed.

All the while, I sat in a hospital waiting room and prayed. I didn't know I could pray so hard for so long. The minutes seemed like hours, the hours like weeks. My baby's existence was in the hands of a few men I barely knew, plus Jesus.

"The surgery was a success. It was a huge success!" Dr. Lieber said to me when it was over. "Yes, a huge success!"

He said he was able to cut away the tumor and all the tissue that was near it to further ensure there were no more tumors left.

"A real success!" he said, beaming as if he'd just won the lottery.

He praised his team of surgeons and specialists, the brave few who had willingly joined him for this Super Surgery to save a young girl's life. He told the same thing to reporters on the air.

The celebration was short-lived.

In what seemed like a near instant, the tumor began to grow back. They'd discovered it by X-ray during a routine post-op checkup, and, once again, we were told we had to act quickly.

Dr. Lieber, the neurologist Dr. Etz, Brit's oncologist, had recruited for the so-called Super Surgery, was re-recruited for the sequel. Brittani's first operation was a right thoracotomy. That surgery was intended to specifically remove all the tumor that was growing on and clinging to her spine. Now, they'd discovered yet another tumor around her spine, and she would require a left thoracotomy to get it, too.

Dr. Lieber said this operation wouldn't be as intense or risky as the first one had been. In fact, he'd do it alone with only an anesthesiologist and a few clinical attendants. But the tumor was growing, he said, and it needed to be removed.

So, only a few months later, I found myself in the same hospital and waiting room, praying the same prayers to my same God.

Deep in thought and conversation with Jesus, I was startled to look up and see Dr. Lieber standing before me. It was as if he had just appeared out of nowhere.

"Doctor?" I asked, confused.

"Tami, we've run into a problem during surgery. It's going to take a little longer than I'd anticipated, but I'm sure everything is going to be okay," he said.

I looked at him blankly, but nothing came out of my mouth.

"Now, try not to worry. I just wanted to come out personally and let you know about the issues. We're going to be in there a while longer. The tumor is completely wrapped around Brittani's spine and entwined in her other organs. Please understand we're on top of things. We're doing everything we can."

The doctor turned and walked away. My stomach fell to the floor. My prayers went into overdrive.

It indeed took longer, much longer than anyone anticipated. At some point, time itself seemed irrelevant, as they say it is in Heaven, a moment being a thousand years or a thousand years being a moment. It seemed as if my whole existence was and would be inside that sterile, cold waiting room.

And then he appeared again.

"The surgery's a success!" he belted out. "We've removed all of the tumor!"

I thanked Dr. Lieber with a quick hug and handshake. I thanked Jesus with a short, silent prayer.

"Your daughter is in recovery," I heard him say as he walked down the hall. "She'll be asleep for a while, but you can see her a little later." I checked Brittani's patient number on the digital update board, and sure enough, she was in recovery.

It was the next day before I saw Dr. Lieber again, this time from Brittani's hospital room, where I'd spent the night in one of the reclining chairs. Brittani was awake and alert but still groggy from the anesthesia and pain medication. We made small talk in between her dozing off.

The doctor came in optimistic and cheery, much like he'd been post-operation. He told Brittani he was going to perform a little exam.

"Move your right foot, okay?" he said.

He waited. Nothing happened.

"Okay, now move your left foot." It didn't move.

The doctor's demeanor changed abruptly. He reached into his lab coat and pulled out a small silver straight pin. He stuck the pin into the bottom of my daughter's right foot.

"Do you feel that, Brittani?" he asked. She looked back at him and slowly shook her head no.

He switched feet and stuck the pin into the sole of her left foot.

"How about that? Can you feel *that*?" Again, she shook her head no.

*Oh my God,* I thought, *she's got no feeling. She's got no feeling in her legs.* My heart turned into NASCAR. I broke into a cold sweat.

At about that same time, a nurse beckoned for the doctor's attention. She took him aside, whispered something, and pointed to the tube that had been inserted into Brittani's chest. I followed her pointing and saw a clear tube filled with a murky liquid. Upon the doctor's order, the nurse removed the fluid and left the hospital room carrying its contents.

"We're going to do some tests," the doctor said. "It appears Brittani had a spinal cord stroke during surgery."

A *what?* I thought. I'd heard of a stroke before, but not a spinal cord stroke. I felt numb. I looked at my daughter, and tears had welled up in her eyes. She lay staring at the ceiling.

"We're going to monitor the spinal cord leakage for the next few days, so she'll be staying here, but we expect it to stop," he said.

Brittani and I said nothing, not knowing *what* to say.

"And she's got some lower-body weakness, which we believe she can overcome," the doctor said.

In a few days, the spinal cord leakage stopped, and Brittani was discharged. We went home. Brittani still didn't have much feeling in her legs or feet, but with assistance from others, she could walk, if only barely.

She'd experienced something called "foot-drop" and had terrible difficulty lifting the front parts of her feet. Whenever she needed to move, it took another person, usually me, to help. She'd put her arms around me, and I'd put mine around her, and we'd shuffle, dancelike, a few steps at a time. It was a world away from running point guard for her varsity basketball team.

Unable to walk up a flight of stairs to her bedroom, Brittani had taken to sleeping on the family room sofa. To get to the

kitchen or bathroom, she traversed the room in my worksta-
tion's office chair, the kind with wheels.

When things didn't improve in a month, we decided to fit
her feet for prostheses. Her physical therapists said that might
improve her overall movement and mobility. Braces would run
from the bottom of her feet up her legs, fastened together with
straps. I thought she would move a little abnormally, but they
would allow her some form of mobility and independence.

As we left the physical therapy office after her fitting, we
were walking through the parking lot in our usual dancing
fashion when, without warning, Brittani screamed from excruciating pain.

"Oh my God, Mom, my back! *My back!*" she yelled and fell
into my arms.

I struggled to get her into the car, her screams not subsiding,
and by the time I'd lifted her into the passenger seat, she was in
agony, in tears. "*My back!*" she continued to cry.

We were a few miles from a local hospital, and I broke every
speed limit trying to get there. I pulled into the emergency
room driveway, ran inside to get an attendant, and explained her
medical history quickly and on the fly.

The ER doctor saw her briefly, gave her some medicine
to dull the pain, and said she'd be alright. I elaborated upon
her condition in great detail, but the doctor explained the pain
away and wrote me a prescription to fill if the pain resurfaced.
As Brittani was wheelchaired back to our car, I took the slip of
paper from his hand and left.

Early the next morning, I woke to Brittani screaming again,
this time from her bed on the family room sofa.

"Mom, I can't move! *I can't move!*"

I leaped out of bed and was beside her nearly instantly.

"What *is* it, baby? *What?*" I said.

"I can't feel my feet! I can't feel my legs!" she shrieked.

I began running my hands up and down her lower torso, from her feet to her shins and calves, up to her thighs, and back down again, all the while yelling, "Can you feel that, Brittani? Can you feel that?!"

"No, Mom, I *can't*. I can't feel *anything!*" she said, panicked.

For some reason, I didn't call for an ambulance, not wanting to deal with another doctor or hospital that didn't understand the complexities or critical nature of her condition. Instead, I called Dr. Lieber. He was the expert, supposedly the only person willing to take a chance on Brittani when we needed it.

In the meantime, while I was on the phone, Brittani suddenly lost feeling and control of her bladder. She said she couldn't feel any sensation there either.

The doctor told us to get her to Children's Hospital ASAP. Within an hour, we were back at Children's Hospital.

"The X-rays suggest she's paralyzed from the chest down," Dr. Lieber said. "From the T4 down."

The T4 thoracic vertebra is in the middle of the spinal column. Above her chest area, Brittani could move her arms and head and talk, but from her chest down, her body was motionless.

"The spinal stroke, in all likelihood, caused the paralysis," the doctor said. "She might be able to recover, but—"

His voice trailed off. He never did finish the sentence.

Dr. Etz, her pediatric oncologist, suggested putting Brittani on Celebrex, a form of chemotherapy. I almost lost it when I heard the word chemo, but he assured me it was being used experimentally for arthritis patients, and some patients' tumor chemistry also responded well.

Still, something in the doctor's next sentence chilled my bones.

"It will give her time," he said.

I looked at him, wanting and needing to hear something more.

"It will give her time," he repeated.

Brittani began to take Celebrex, and, in fact, it did her body well. The pain in her back mostly subsided. There was less discomfort in her lower extremities. While my daughter was now confined to a wheelchair, she'd learned to live with it, to pilot her way around the house or down the street. She could take in the occasional movie, and we went to church together every Sunday. With her wheelchair packed in the back seat, we'd drive to Los Angeles on vacation. We went to Magic Mountain. It seemed that over a short period of time, we went everywhere.

She gradually adapted to her life on wheels like a great athlete would, and I adapted alongside her. We'd enrolled in a wonderful rehabilitation program that taught her—but mostly me—the only limitation she faced was what I, or better yet, my fears, were not allowing her to do. Brittani could do everything she did before, just in a slightly different way.

She went back to school after missing half a year and still graduated with a 3.5 GPA. She began attending parties and social events with her friends. On weekends, we'd sit on the couch together, laughing, talking, and watching Tyler Perry's stage plays.

My faith in God had never been greater than during this time. I felt in my heart He's got this. Sure, my daughter was confined to a wheelchair, but it seemed like our journey together was moving forward. It was a different kind of trip than I'd imagined, of course, but things were okay. Things seemed like they were going to be okay.

For two and a half years, Brittani enjoyed a real sense of normalcy in her life. She enrolled in classes at a local college. She hung out with family and friends. She enjoyed most things a young woman enjoys, and she planned for her future.

However, there was always a nagging, lingering feeling within me, an uncomfortable sense deep inside that kept me awake most nights.

"It will give her time," Dr. Etz had said when he prescribed Celebrex.

Indeed, it had given us time, but I always wondered how much.

I was driving home from the grocery store one afternoon in early 2009, listening to the radio, when a newscast mentioned the actor John Travolta's son, Jett, had passed away suddenly at age 17. He was rumored to have been autistic, and he died as the result of a seizure, the reporter said.

I remember thinking he was a little younger than Brittani.

As I sat at a red light, I began to cry. I never knew Jett Travolta. And like most people, I only knew his parents from the movies. But yet, I began to weep so hard that I had to pull over when the light changed and try to get my composure. I found myself praying for his soul and the protection of his family.

It seemed the young man's death was sudden and without warning. They were on vacation, the report said, somewhere in the Bahamas. He'd had a seizure, and without warning, he was gone forever.

*The Travolta family did not have the gift of time*, I thought.

My thoughts quickly turned to my daughter and to the many remarkable life events we'd shared since she'd become paralyzed. If Brittani were to perish suddenly, without warning, without the chance to laugh again or even say goodbye, it would be worse, I thought, than if she slowly faded away. To be together on a beach one minute and, boom, gone the next would be unfathomable for a parent.

I sat on the side of the road, wiping away the tears from my eyes, talking out loud to God, thanking Him for giving me the past couple of years with my beautiful daughter.

"This is the gift of time," He said back to me.

By the tone of His voice, I understood He meant for me to use it wisely.

I had never before told Brittani her prognosis was, in all likelihood, terminal. I didn't want to believe it myself, and I certainly did not want her to even consider that possibility. I didn't want her to spend one breathing moment thinking about dying. I only wanted her to focus on living today and planning for her tomorrow.

But that afternoon, after returning home, I sat down with my daughter and told her the truth. I told her how lucky I was to have been blessed with her in my life and how happy and proud she had always made me. I said that while she had been given a raw deal, we were going to make the most of our days on earth together.

I never got around to telling her about death or even mentioning that dreadful word. Instead, we talked about life and living it to the fullest. I shared with her how I heard God say,

"You've been given the gift of time." I now understand that we should live every day like it's our final one, embracing every fleeting moment because the present is the gift.

We shared how we've been truly and wonderfully blessed with the Gift of Time.

"I like that, Mom," Brittani said. "The Gift of Time."

We were at the local Dollar Store one day, a favorite pastime of Brittani's and mine. Sometimes, just to goof off and lift our spirits, we'd up and spend an hour or so browsing for nothing in particular, stocking up on junk food and knick-knacks. We'd move through the aisles together, with her in her wheelchair and me right beside her, pointing out items and just enjoying our time out of the house.

We were at the cash register. Brittani, always independent, had brought her own money and was checking out. I was behind her, waiting for my turn.

As she scanned my daughter's items, the cashier stopped and began to look deeply into Brittani's eyes.

"Oh, my God. You are so beautiful, and there's something about you," the cashier said. "There's this beauty. There's this light emanating from you."

The cashier looked at Brittani. Then she glanced back at me. And then back at Brittani.

"May I just come over and hug you?" she asked.

"Yeah," Brittani said softly.

The cashier left her post, walked around the conveyor belt, bent down, and wrapped her arms around Brittani.

"I hear God speaking very loudly right now," the cashier said.

I looked around at other customers waiting to check out, unsure what was happening. The cashier kept Brittani in her tight embrace.

"God is telling me to tell you not to be afraid," the cashier said. "He says your life and your journey are meant to inspire people. Continue on, my girl. Do not be afraid. *Do not be afraid.*"

The cashier loosened her grip and took a step backward, away from Brittani and her wheelchair, but she continued to gaze at her.

"There are three angels around you," she said. "The mother Mary and two other angels."

The entire Dollar Store grew quiet. For a moment, all activity had ceased.

"They're here to protect you, my love," said the cashier. "Do not be afraid. Your light is meant to inspire others."

Brittani and I were both emotional and left speechless at this incredible encounter. And if that wasn't enough of a miracle encounter, as soon as we left the store and settled in the car to head home, my phone rang. It was Dr. Etz.

"We found an alternative treatment for Brittani that will not require chemotherapy. How soon can you get to the hospital?" Dr. Etz said very excitedly on the other end.

"Brittani and I are in the car now and headed your way," I said as I made a U-turn.

"Good, good. We'll talk in my office," he said.

Brit and I looked at each other and instinctively said, "Thank you, Jesus!" We headed straight for the hospital, singing the praises of God and shouting the whole way.

CHAPTER 9

# MODERN-DAY STORY OF JOB

*"Because you are more than a conqueror, you must go through more than a conqueror goes through, but the end result is always victory."*

–Unknown

The dollar store cashier was right. Brittani did indeed inspire others. Her resolve, her determination, and the way she managed her battle with this illness with dignity inspired others beyond what she ever imagined.

Like the woman at that checkout counter, I, too, felt my baby had angels working for her. Grammy and Grandpa, both of whom had passed by now, were probably two of them. My dad and sister Jeannine, I imagined, were the others. From what I surmised, Brittani had an entire angelic army watching out for her.

But on earth, even angels have limitations. Brittani had another spinal cord stroke, and the Celebrex was no longer working. The cancer had found other pathways around it, and tumors began growing rapidly again.

This time it affected her right hand, her writing hand, the hand she once used to push the ball up the court. Her legs were already gone, and her hands were now failing. She had begun to enter decline.

When that cashier spoke to Brittani, she seemed to look through her as if God Himself was speaking to her. It brightened her spirits so much because the past few months were the worst we'd experienced since she was diagnosed. And when Dr. Etz's call came in, I just knew it was a miracle in the making.

I repeated Dr. Etz's words in my head over and over again, "I believe we've found an alternative treatment."

It was the glimmer of hope we prayed for in a sea of despair. I didn't know what he meant by "alternative," but at this point, I'd have tried *anything* if it held some measure of promise.

Dr. Etz described the drug to us as a natural form of chemotherapy, an injection into her system of organic biological material that, in previous tests at least, had shown promise in slowing—and sometimes stopping altogether—the growth of tumors. The doctor was careful in his word choice not to provide us with any sense of false hope, but to Brittani and me, *any* hope was golden, false or not.

"Let's try it," Brittani said. She looked at me. I hesitated, if only for a millisecond. The uncomfortable idea of my beautiful baby being part of a medical experiment hit me hard. My Brittani was nobody's lab rat. But then, nothing conventional had worked, and per Dr. Etz, we were out of all other options.

"Let's try it," I said and glanced back at Brittani. We exchanged slight smiles at the unexpected ray of confidence.

With time, prayer, and lots of hope, the injections seemed to make things better. The tumors, if not retreating or disappearing, had indeed slowed their once-rapid growth. For a while, she was not getting worse, which, when you're desperate, is just as cherished as getting better.

It was another Gift of Time, the alternative treatment. There were no guarantees, of course, but it bought us a couple more years together, a sacred time during which we saw and experienced the absolute hand of God in many forms. Then it, too, stopped working.

One day, the experimental injections ceased slowing down the tumors, and they began growing again on her spine, this time with a vengeance. Yet, no one could explain why.

The tumors began to take a noticeable form, as they caused scoliosis, a curvature of her spine so pronounced it altered the way she was able to sit in her wheelchair. It distorted her upper body. It would inevitably take a toll on her vital internal organs, we were warned, which would subsequently begin to cause serious complications of their own.

Already paralyzed from the chest down, Brittani was now forced to wear a scoliosis body brace to try to correct the curvature. The tumors she'd had, Dr. Etz said, had corroded her spine to the point where it nearly severed itself.

This time, the doctor seemed less optimistic than when he introduced us to the experimental treatment. I could see concern, maybe even fear, in Dr. Etz's eyes.

"I want you to understand," he said, "she's already paralyzed, the tumors on her spine are growing again rapidly, and even the best-case scenario carries a dire prognosis, one you're not going to be happy with."

I looked at him intently, searching for meaning.

I was waiting for the payoff line, the "but, if …" that never came.

Looking directly at Brit, he said, "Brittani, I'm afraid there's nothing else we can do."

She continued looking at him, and he at her. In the silence in his office, I could hear nothing but our breathing.

"I mean, I'm afraid we've exhausted all of our options."

More silence.

"I'm so, so sorry, Brittani and Tami. I'm so sorry."

In the days that followed, Brittani's hair fell out completely. She was unable to eat much and endured endless diarrhea, which caused her to grow gravely thin. Losing her mobility, she was forced to drop out of college. But even within those darkened days, her spirit shone through in a most fascinating, miraculous, and unexpected way.

A short time later, and out of the blue, Brittani reconnected with her father, Sherman.

Sometime that summer, the two became pen pals, exchanging letters back and forth. Sherman had been out of our lives for many years, thankfully, I must admit.

By then, my life had changed 360 degrees. I'd moved on and eventually married my grade school sweetheart, who had a one-year-old son, Christian. Together, we had two children, Bri, Brian II, and Tiki, who came into our lives weeks after Brit's initial diagnosis.

My life was now light years from the life I lived with Sherman. As a matter of fact, looking back, it felt much like someone else's life as I no longer identified with the young girl whose husband murdered a young lady weeks before giving birth to Brittani.

I must admit, it greatly concerned me that Sherman had re-entered Brittani's life at this point. I was anxious about their relationship, unsure of Sherman's reason for pursuing a relationship with a daughter he hadn't seen since infancy. I honestly thought that part of my life was dead forever.

In a delicate way, I tried to prepare Brittani for her father, for the inevitable letdown and the eventual pain Sherman always seemed to leave behind. Was he still on heroin? I asked myself. Had he killed any additional young mothers? Why would a man so self-centered suddenly want a friendship with a daughter he'd abandoned two decades before?

In so many ways, I hadn't even processed the fact that he was a murderer. I'd learned how to dissociate so well that my former life felt much like a dream or, better yet, a nightmare. The reality of that period never felt completely processed in my mind.

"Honey, just don't expect anything," I told her. "Don't expect too much from him."

Sherman had broken my heart. I'd kill him myself if he broke Brittani's, too. I am not talking about a theoretical kill either; I would li-ter-al-ly kill him with my bare hands. Remember, things buried alive don't die; they just fester.

But Brittani knew her physical condition. She realized her prognosis. And I could understand her wanting to complete her identity. So, I had no choice, and I gave her the space to discover more of herself through a relationship with her father.

I'd read the letters from Sherman as Brit shared them with me and found them to be quite normal between a dad and his daughter. He shared details with her about his side of the family and introduced her to her ancestry. He'd say Brittani was part of their family, a family she'd never met, and explained where some of her traits and talents derived. Her artistic ability was definitely in her DNA, directly from him. He connected with her through their commonality. It was truly sweet to see this side of him, the tender side who loved Brit to his core, the true essence of him, not the demons in him I'd come to know. She truly brought out the best in him.

"So you like to draw? So do I! You get that from *me!*" he wrote.

"And you're interested in architecture? So am I! You get that from *me!*"

Knowing Brittani's frail health and naturally loving soul, I was on heightened alert and extremely mama-bearish about her. Her newly formed relationship with Sherman caused me much angst. As a result, I dealt with emotions I hadn't felt or experienced in what felt like a lifetime ago. Was he *playing* her? If so, for *what?*

Nevertheless, Brittani and Sherman began to really bond. He'd call her daughter, and she'd call him Dad. I was worried about it all, just not sure where it was heading, and I definitely never revealed the murder to her. It just didn't seem right to do so. What would it benefit? There was no need for her to experience more trauma on top of a terminal cancer diagnosis, I thought. So, I remained silent.

Months into their correspondence, I got a phone call from Sherman. It was the first time I'd heard his voice in many, many years. He sounded somewhat different, sober maybe, but definitely less of a wild young man. He sounded, dare I say, adult-like and compassionate.

I told him Brittani had really taken to him and seemed to enjoy having him in her life, if only long-distance. I told him what an athlete she was, how smart and talented she was, how beautiful she was inside and out, and how she was an absolute angel. I told him about her health issues, too, how what started as back pain had now, over the years, metastasized into scoliosis, paralysis, cancer, and chemotherapy.

*"What?!"* I heard Sherman nearly scream into the receiver. In all the letters Brittani had written to him, she had obviously not mentioned her illness. She vaguely mentioned some limitations or struggles she had, but he had no idea she was so sick.

I heard a very different Sherman on the end of that phone line that day.

"I've lived my whole life without having empathy, Tami," he said, "and without giving a damn about anyone else. Now this. My baby girl has cancer?!"

He took some time on the other end to collect himself, so I held the phone and respectfully gave him that time.

"My baby girl may die," he said quietly. I can't say for certain, but I believe Sherman was crying. The last time I'd heard him cry, he was hiding in the kitchen cabinets.

"I've never cared much for anyone else before," Sherman continued. "But now I'm scared for Brittani. I don't want my daughter to suffer, Tami. My baby doesn't deserve this. I deserve to be where she is; I deserve to suffer greatly, but she doesn't deserve it. She is so sweet and precious to me."

I sat there and listened. I didn't say much at all. It seemed like Sherman needed to unload, so I very patiently allowed him. He thanked me for taking great care of our daughter all these years and for being a good mom to her. He said it was great that Brittani had a mom like me who loved and cared for her so well, especially now that he knew what he knew.

He never acknowledged the bad times we'd shared, the drug abuse, the murder of that young woman and mom, the mental and physical abuse I endured at his hands, the neglect, the lack of child support payments for our daughter's entire existence. He never told me if he'd gotten sober or not. He never went there, and neither did I. At that moment, none of that seemed important.

Sherman thanked me again, this time even more profusely. We said our goodbyes, and he gently hung up the phone. For a moment, I listened to the stillness on the line, then gently hung up, too. I took several minutes to process our conversation and the compassion I felt coming from Sherman.

*Wow*, I thought. After all this time, we ended here. It seemed organic.

It seemed real and all right.

About a month later, I got a phone call from Sherman's mother, Mary. As with her son, I hadn't heard her voice in just as many years, yet I immediately sensed unease and sorrow when she spoke her first syllable.

"Tami, Sherman died. He passed away unexpectedly," she said.

I sank. I said nothing.

"He had pneumonia. He'd been in the hospital. He wouldn't take the medication. He said he didn't want to be on all that and passed away," she said. I heard Sherman's mother sobbing on the other end about her son, just as Sherman had done a month before when he learned the news about his daughter.

"I just—I just thought I should tell you," she said. I gave her my sincere condolences and promised I would let Brittani know. We said our goodbyes and hung up.

I closed my eyes and said a prayer—for Sherman's soul, for the comfort of his mother, for his other kids, and for Brittani. I stared at the wall for what seemed like forever, weak from the news and not even sure what emotions I was feeling. What I did know is that the Sherman chapter of my life had come to a sudden, complete, and unexpected end. I didn't weep right away.

In fact, I initially felt devoid of emotion and was very likely in complete shock. For me, Sherman had died long, long ago. But for *our* daughter, the story had just begun.

I walked into the next room to break the news to Brittani.

In the Old Testament, there's a story about a man named Job. He was a righteous man and a favorite in the eyes of God, but he was tested mercilessly to see if his faith would endure. At some point, I began to believe Job and I were kindred spirits.

It began with breaking the news about Sherman's death to Brittani, just as they'd begun to get to know each other. And like boils on Job's body, it sprouted and spread from there.

I had contracted pneumonia, diagnosed with it the very same day Sherman passed away from the same affliction, and from it resurfaced serious heart complications. As a younger woman, I'd undergone heart surgery that was botched, and I'd refused to address any coronary issues since then.

I recovered from the pneumonia a couple of months later, sure enough, but while out having lunch with my husband and kids, I began to feel my heart racing. Its normal thump-thump, thump-thump beat was replaced by a near-constant buzzing that felt and sounded like the vibration of hummingbird wings.

By the time we'd gotten the kids home, I assured them everything was okay *but* that I needed to visit the emergency room to have my heart checked out. Stunned, the kids didn't know what to say or do. They had no idea my heart was racing until I told them.

I soon arrived at the hospital emergency room, and by this time, my heart was in full tachycardia at 181 beats per minute.

For reference, the normal resting heart rate is between 60 and 100 beats per minute.

In the hospital, they shocked my heart twice that evening to get it back to a normal sinus rhythm. Once the medicine hit my system, I felt like I was falling backward through a never-ending tunnel at an uncontrollable high rate of speed. I literally thought I was going to die! Once they stabilized my heart, I was discharged with orders to follow up with the cardio doctor.

While I was ecstatic to spend the holidays at home with the kids and family, we were saddened by the sudden passing of our family dog, Bishop. We'd had the dog for ten years, and he was a constant companion for our family. This, on top of everything else, was excruciating, and we ALL took it very hard.

After Christmas and during a rather routine doctor's follow-up to the pneumonia, the doctors discovered my lungs were filled with fluid, probably left over from the pneumonia. My lung function was only 37 percent of what it should have been. A biopsy revealed it could possibly be lung cancer. To make matters worse, or possibly because of the shock from the news, my heart palpitations began again but now went into overdrive.

Within days, a lung biopsy was scheduled for a clear diagnosis. For the short time I was in the hospital, Brittani had been admitted to a hospice facility one block away for round-the-clock care as I was her primary caregiver.

While in the hospital, my heart went into tachycardia again, exceeding 180 beats per minute. My nurse very calmly peeked his head into my room and asked if I was okay.

I said, "Yes, except my heart is racing."

He said, "Yeah, I kinda noticed. Let me call the on-call cardiologist."

The next thing I knew, my room was filled with medical staff, and my heart was being shocked back to normal sinus rhythm. That familiar feeling of falling backward into the never-ending tube came back.

As I lay there, I was thinking about my baby girl in the hospice facility who needed me to get better and what she, my husband, or other kids would do if I died. I also thought about how this couldn't possibly be my life.

Once my heart was stabilized, the cardiologist consulted with me and told me very bluntly, "You need to have the heart ablation surgery soon, or you will die from this." How's that for a sobering reality on top of everything else?

Exactly a month later, I was back in the hospital for the heart ablation procedure—a procedure to ablate the extra pathway in the chamber of my heart, which was causing it to work overtime. In my case, from the botched surgery years earlier, the extra pathway allowed incorrect electrical signals to cause an abnormal heart rhythm. The surgeon successfully ablated the extra pathway and inserted catheters through my heart's blood vessels to map the heart's electrical signals.

The surgery took place in early March, marking a season filled with many trials. One hardship after another unfolded, making our journey mirror that of Job himself.

Not even a couple of weeks after the heart ablation, my husband developed pulmonary embolisms—blood clots—in both lungs, which doctors termed a saddle embolism, and he veered suddenly toward near-death. It was, in fact, Brittani who'd noticed his labored breathing and insisted on getting him checked out.

Her acuity saved his life, as the doctors said the blood clots would have killed him within hours. He underwent emergency surgery to remove the blood clots and remained in the hospital for several days. Our 17-year-old daughter Bri had to step up and completely care for the household during this time, from grocery shopping to cooking, cleaning, and caring for her younger siblings and Brit as well as me and her dad. She resiliently stepped into the role and took care of business!

After my husband was released from the hospital, our car's sunroof suddenly shattered out of nowhere, spewing broken glass everywhere. If it all weren't so serious, it would have seemed comical. But I recognized this to be absolute spiritual warfare, and the enemy had one goal—to take us all out!!

Or perhaps it was just another little Job-like test thrown our way. In any regard, it is ONLY by the grace and favor of God that we limped out of all of these attacks or tests alive.

The next time Brittani was enrolled in hospice care wasn't because I was hospitalized and she needed someone to watch over her. The next time was at the recommendation of Dr. Etz, who'd concluded her health had deteriorated to a point of no return. He recommended home hospice care, as he didn't believe she'd be physically able to travel to the weekly appointments from home again.

This was just a week after the saddle embolism emergency and three weeks from my heart ablation. When I tell you we were all ravaged by the severe attacks coming at us, we couldn't tell one day from the next. It was either jumping into action (fight or flight) or totally succumbing to all of this. We all stepped up and fought with several limps from this battle.

We seemed to be getting hit with blow after blow and couldn't even come up for air before the next blow would hit, each one more intense than the previous. Dr. Etz and his colleagues, Ann, our nurse, and Regina, the social worker, had grown particularly close to Brittani over her years of treatment with them. It was an emotional day when they said their good-byes and escorted her from Dr. Etz's office. Although no one said it, we knew it would be her last visit.

On the drive home, Brittani insisted on stopping at Walmart. She liked to stock up on snacks and other odds and ends. That evening, as we pushed Brittani in her wheelchair around Walmart, I noticed she was drifting in and out of con-sciousness, probably from the incredible number of meds inside her. She'd had to take a higher dose to prepare for the trip to the doctor's office due to the incredible amount of pain she was in at this point.

"You can't stay awake, baby," I whispered to her at one point, "So let's get what you need and go home." She readily agreed.

Once home and inside her room, Brittani was preparing for a visit from her younger cousins while I was putting the grocer-ies away when she fell from her wheelchair face-first, and my youngest daughter Tiki miraculously caught her.

When I heard her scream a very panicked "MOM!" from Brit's room, I knew immediately that something was very wrong.

I came running, only to find Brit unconscious and in her sister's hands. She had literally fallen face-first into her six-year-old sister's arms, who was struggling to keep her from hitting the floor. I grabbed Brit, turned her on her back, and laid her limp body on the floor as I called 9-1-1.

As our family members were knocking on our front door, I was on the phone with the 911 operator. They came inside and discovered a terrifying scene. She's dying, they thought, and so did I.

I told the girls to leave. I wanted them to leave before the ambulance arrived. Brittani was very adamant about never wanting ANYONE to see her like that, and I had to honor her wishes regardless of how I felt about it.

Very reluctantly, they left, but I know they were traumatized. My heart still feels extremely heavy for each of the girls to this day.

The paramedics could not revive Brit at first. I watched in horror as they tried to resuscitate my baby once, then twice, then load her onto a stretcher and quickly wheel her into the ambulance.

I grabbed my car keys and followed the lights and blaring siren to the all-too-familiar hospital emergency room, where both my husband and I had just been with dire emergencies of our own days and weeks before.

I prayed and cried out to Jesus all the way there. Talk about desperate and fervent prayers—I promise you, they don't come any more desperate than that!

In the emergency room, they shot Brit up with a medicine called Naloxone, which amazingly revived her to not only the point of consciousness but to relative normalcy instantly. When I rushed into the room, Brittani seemed more embarrassed by the episode than concerned by it.

I hugged her tightly, thanking God for answering my panicked prayers, crying tears of relief, disbelief, yes, and joy, and holding her in my arms once more.

That evening, when Brittani was permitted to leave, I drove her home and sat beside her all night, watching her breathe and taking in those borrowed hours from the Gift of Time.

On Earth, everything has an expiration date.

A week later, Brittani and I both knew our Gift of Time was about to expire.

By then, Brittani would sleep most of the day but awaken suddenly to tell me about these incredible conversations she was having with God and the incredible things He was teaching her. I'd listen intently and take detailed notes. I instinctively knew this was a very sacred time, and I wanted to hear about everything God was telling Brit in this hour, as she was now the closest to Him.

She'd fall back asleep again for more hours, her breathing soft, almost imperceptible, until she'd pop awake again with another story to tell.

*"So, we're in heaven, and they're having this big celebration, this huge, wonderful party. And it's all for me, Mom, it's all for me! Everybody there is so happy to see me.*

*"Grammy is making food, Mom, and she's such a wonderful cook. She makes the best grilled cheese sandwiches and gives the tightest, most loving, and most comforting hugs that make me feel like everything is okay.*

*"And Grandpa is there, and he's letting me play with the keys to the church, this huge church he's in charge of. He keeps them in his pockets and jiggles them around! I love playing with the keys.*

*"And my grandpa Richmond is there, and guess what?! We both love drinking black coffee! It's so wonderfully delicious, Mom, don't you agree? We always clink cups and laugh.*

*"And Mom, my Auntie Jeannine is there, too! Oh, how I love her. She's the best friend ever! We're always dancing together and running around.*

*"It's such a wonderful place, Mom, with such wonderful people. Oh, we're so blessed to have such wonderful people.*

*"And everyone loves you, Mom. They all love you dearly.*

*"And they all tell me to tell you the same thing. Every one of them says to tell you this. Do you want to know what it is, Mom? Do you really want to know what they tell me to tell you?*

*"Here's what they say, Mom:*

*"They say you can overcome everything that's coming at you. That's what they all say.*

*"They say to tell your mom everything that's coming at her, she already has it within her to overcome."*

---

**Journal Entry**

*March 29, 2012*

**Passover**

"But rejoice inasmuch as you participate in the sufferings of Christ, so that you may be overjoyed when HIS Glory is revealed" (1 Peter 4:13, NIV).

Gentle reminder: If you suffer with Him, you will reign with Him. Continue to look for the goodness of God while you go through this valley. It's a great day in the Lord. If you woke up this morning, you are among the blessed. #GiftofTime

CHAPTER 10

# DYING TO LIVE

*"My brokenness cost me everything.*
*My surrender cost me even more."*

—Tami Franklin

Rock bottom is very sacred ground, even if it is uncomfortable. It's where you pray your most desperate prayers. It's where you cry, wail, and even scream out your most raw and honest tears that you didn't even know were inside you. Rock bottom is a dark, damp place most people spend their lives trying to avoid. We may fall far and long, but human nature and culture say try your hardest not to hit rock bottom. No one wants to go there.

I finally hit complete rock bottom when Brittani died. Such a sentence has no place being a thought, much less being real. The gap between her dreams and our reality had been closed. In one sense, my life was over; in another, my life had just begun.

When a person is in a place so deep and dark as to feel like it's their personal everlasting hell on earth, that's where you've got to meet them. You have to descend into that hell right where they are and speak life to them, or tomorrow might never come.

One must face-plant into the earth if they are going to someday fly. One must allow oneself to experience and acknowledge every single wave of emotion that rises to the surface. Only then will growth and healing begin. Growth and healing are often more painful than the initial wound, but it is very much part of the process and essential to the cycles of grief.

While it may be true that the best things in life are free, it is also true that living your most meaningful life will cost you absolutely everything! This I now know.

Shortly after her passing, I was casually scrolling through Facebook when I came across my neighbor Ashley's post. In it, she was asking people to pray for a friend of hers.

The woman she wrote about had been through hell, it seemed, a succession of health catastrophes nobody should have to endure. Her friend had just undergone heart and lung surgery and was in the healing stage, but still fragile. The woman's husband had experienced a blood clot that had almost cost him his life. And now this lady's daughter, who had been ill for a long time, had passed away.

Ashley's Facebook words pleaded for internal peace for this woman, for her well-being.

"That poor, poor woman," I thought. "How horrific. How tragic."

I closed my eyes to offer up a brief prayer for the woman when I reread the Facebook post. I read it again a third time.

My God, she's talking about *me*!

She's talking about *my* life. Ashley was asking her Facebook friends to pray for *me*.

They say when you're in the eye of a hurricane, you don't notice the chaos around you. Inside the eye, it's calm. Quiet, even, eerily so. Things seem absurdly normal inside the eye. At the edge of the storm, though, on the outside in the high winds, people everywhere are running for cover, locking themselves inside their shelters and witnessing destruction while hoping to save themselves.

Tears welled up in my eyes. I set my phone down and stared blankly ahead.

Yes, it was me whom Ashley was asking to be prayed for. Within the years of Brittani's illness and months of her deteriorating health, I'd somehow been able to sever myself from the terrible reality my neighbor and doubtless others saw as my endless trauma.

Emotionally, I'd kept my mind inside the hurricane's eye, where it was nice and sunny. Psychologically, I'd remained inside some comfortable enough storm shelter as all hell swirled around me.

In the days following Brittani's passing, I stayed in a mental cocoon (God's amazing hedge of protection), numbly powered by the Holy Spirit, going through the motions of what was required of a mother who'd lost her firstborn child.

We asked our pastor, Bishop Thom, to make her service less of a funeral and more of a celebration of life. He complied wonderfully, relating to the small crowd in attendance the spiritual messages of Brittani's final days and her angelic optimism that she was going to a better place, a place without wheelchairs and pain and struggle. It was where healing occurred and prayers were answered.

My family and friends flew to Arizona from all over to comfort those who knew and loved Brit. We had loud dinner parties.

We laughed and cried together. My cell phone chimed continuously for days on end with condolence calls and thoughtful text messages.

When a loved one passes away, survivors hear a lot of "If you need anything at all, just_____," but in the days following Brit's passing, that trite phrase never seemed to lose its magic. The words gave me hope and something to anchor to.

But eventually, there are planes for family members to catch to return to their homes. Slowly, the phone calls fade, and text messages dwindle back to their previous frequency. The doorbell stops ringing. And the check-ins fade into nothingness.

With my baby gone and the great hurricane over, I was left by myself to survey the damage, to view with unfiltered eyes the pain that would be my new life.

My lung and heart surgeries, while successful, had taken a toll of their own in addition to all of the medications I'd been prescribed. I'd gained a lot of weight and was almost 300 pounds as a result of the prednisone due to the pneumonia and serious inflammation.

Within a month of Brittani's passing, I was severely depressed, bedridden, and alone during the daytime hours. My husband was back at work, and the kids were back to school.

This proved to be a toxic combination. I, too, felt as if I wanted to die, but there were others in my life for whom I needed to live. My husband needed his wife, and our kids still needed their mom, probably more than ever.

We all grieved the loss of Brit and the reality of the totality of all we'd been through to that point. It was a period of complete trauma and devastation, and sadly, that doesn't even begin to scratch the surface of it all. There was no guide on how to get back to normal. I wondered what was even normal anymore. We all struggled to regain our footing on a foundation that was never truly solid to begin with—a foundation that had been cracked long before it crumbled.

Yet, I rested in knowing that the God of our creation is also the God of our last resort. I couldn't let go of the thought that He'd never ask me to suffer this greatly without a higher purpose on the other side.

It's a thought that has remained with me to this day. With Brittani now with Him, she resides forever in paradise. For me, paradise would have to wait. I closed my eyes and asked for His help. "Jesus," I prayed, "please help me. Please, please help me."

My savior responded directly, boldly.

I remember what Jesus said to me while I lay bedridden:

*Tami, I slowed you down long enough for you to take a look at yourself. You're in this bed because I want you to finally examine your life.*

*You've busied yourself with your work. You've busied yourself with taking care of Brittani, your husband, your kids, and many other people simply for the asking. You've given everybody else 2000% of yourself, yet you've never looked out for yourself or come to me for help.*

*You are broken, Tami. You're a shattered image of a daughter of God. I slowed you down—I allowed you to lie in this bed, unable to walk or care for yourself—to give you time to reflect, to give you an opportunity to mend, to see yourself as you really are, and for once realize you cannot do ANY of this without Me.*

*Look at yourself, my daughter. You're a shell of who you were called to be, of whom I need you to be.*

*Your life is precious, Tami—and I need you to know that. I know your thoughts, my love, and I know you want something much different from your current reality. Brittani is with Me. She's safe and healthy and happy forever with Me.*

*Now it's time for you to heal. Now, it's time for you to get well.*

*Now is the time for you to live the life you always desired and the one I ordained for you, Tami. Now is the time.*

I'd like to say that Jesus' words changed everything immediately. But God works in mysterious ways, and often much slower than what we may want and think we need.

I battled grief and depression for several months, most of which were spent in bed. I grieved, grieved again, and then grieved more. I cried and wept, cried and wept, cried and wept for everything that was wrong and out of order in my life. Everything that was out of order and needed healing soured even more after my daughter's passing.

A sobering reality hit me. I lost Brittani. My mother-in-law, Annette, suddenly passed away 10 months later, my second marriage ended a short while after, and the person I once thought I'd be married to for a lifetime not only wanted reimbursement for my daughter's burial plot and funeral expenses in our divorce settlement, but it was also granted. My husband of nearly 20 years, my grade school sweetheart, the one who used to give me butterflies every time I saw him as a young girl, was now at war with me.

This was *extreme* rock bottom for me, and where I believe I crossed over into the realm of severe dissociation. It was both a blessing and a curse. A blessing because it saved and shielded my brain from believing this was all a reality. A curse because I was now severely detached from most reality and often emotionally disconnected from physical presence.

I didn't know a human could hurt or cry so much. I felt a pain that no words could describe. I lay in bed feeling sorry for myself, day after day, praying for some sort of miracle, some otherworldly sign that times would be changing.

And then I met a man from Ghana.

This man, Pastor Simon, knew nothing about me except the few items I'd posted on Facebook. He had obviously gleaned a thumbnail understanding of the loss of my daughter. He had perceptibly assumed I was a woman in crisis. He wasn't pushy. He didn't ask for anything. He didn't claim to be a Nigerian Prince or anything that might signal red flags.

Instead, he simply began to send me prayers he'd written and scripture passages. They'd be sitting in my inbox each morning, beautiful praises to God, glorifying the Lord for His goodness, asking Him to protect me in my time of need.

His prayers met me where I was—in the pit. They touched my very soul. The man from Ghana could not have known how broken and desperate I was, yet … he did. He seemed to have a keen and distinct insight into what plagued my soul.

After a short while, I finally responded and thanked him.

"Listen, I don't know who or where you are, although I think it's somewhere in America," he said in his reply. "I just know that God, for some reason, has been giving me messages to give to you." Again, he asked for nothing in return.

For a year and a half, we corresponded. He'd send a prayer he said was for me, whatever the Lord had placed on his heart. I'd reply. He'd send me a Bible verse or a compelling short story, and I'd thank him for it. It became a matter of routine. I began to expect to hear from him each day, excited at what might be in my inbox the next time I checked. He never disappointed.

Throughout my grief, my mourning period for Brittani, and my bedridden state of poor mental and physical health, Pastor Simon from Ghana was always there. I'd wake up each day, painfully aware my daughter was gone, but then I'd check Facebook, and, sure enough, he'd have sent a few words of encouragement.

His digital presence altered my outlook on life and God; it made me *want* to live another day, if only to see what God had shared with him to send next for me.

Slowly, the eagerness to see his next messages replaced, ever so slightly, the sting of losing Brittani. His prayers were like medicine to my aching heart and broken soul, a sort of nectar from Africa I'd long to taste every day.

With time, I got out of bed more often and felt sorry for myself less and less. I began, slowly but assuredly, to live again. The pain of loss still stung, but it began to be balanced with a purpose for living and the word of God. Like a caterpillar morphing into a butterfly, my metamorphosis had begun.

With time, my physical well-being improved, and my spiritual awakening continued. I knew it was time to begin to clean up my life when I was strong enough to endure what I knew was coming next: beginning the actual work of emotional healing and breaking free from everything that kept me broken.

The man from Ghana helped me realize the words God had spoken to me earlier: *"Now is the time for you to live the life you always desired to live, Tami. Now is the time."*

I was ready for a new chapter in my life. It was time to begin again.

I began grief counseling, which was something I'd never done before. At first, my counselor and I proceeded slowly, earning each other's trust as I began to share my deepest, darkest hours and secrets as she listened, mostly silently and without judgment. With time, I increasingly opened up to her, confiding my heartfelt desire to feel whole again.

We'd talk, discuss different scenarios, and imagine how it would all turn out, how life tomorrow might be better than today.

Slowly but very surely, I began to come alive. With counseling, I began to feel good about myself again, almost like I felt as a young girl when Mr. Mobley would commend me for my writing ability. Yes, it'd been quite a long time since I felt alive; it felt like almost a whole lifetime. I didn't quite know what lay ahead, but I could certainly see the horizon, and this time it wasn't another oncoming train.

Throughout my awakening and healing, I knew Brittani was watching from above. In her earthly life, she understood very clearly that I was fraying at the seams for many years. From beyond, I could feel my baby telling me to be strong, to not fall back into my previous life.

I could also hear Brittani whispering to me to move forward. She told me she had found the courage to let go and answer the higher calling of her life, to put her eternity into the hands of the Lord. She said I could, too, and that if I trusted in God, He would secure my freedom on earth just as He'd done for her in Heaven. She visited me often in my dreams to pass along these messages of encouragement and hope.

As frightening a time as it was, I soldiered forth with Jesus only a prayer away. This is when I truly learned and experienced Him as MY Personal Lord and Savior.

Day by day ... step by step ... moment by moment, my strength, courage, determination, and stamina increased greatly. For the first time in my life, I knew I was going to heal and finally be free. I thanked God continuously.

---

**Journal Entry**

*December 5, 2014, 3 a.m.*

**Whisper**

Now that you've sat in the pain and know what you never knew before, start writing! There's work YET to do! Your suffering has **NOT** been in vain. It was always for a higher and greater purpose. That **IS** the gift, you know that now. Get to work and know that I am still with you.

CHAPTER 11

# UN-BROKEN—THE REAL STORY

*"We were born to make manifest the glory of God that is within us. It's not just in some of us; it's in everyone. And as we let our own light shine, we unconsciously give other people permission to do the same."*

—Marianne Williamson, *A Return to Love*

F or years, I attempted to share my story, but I couldn't bring myself to do it successfully. It was because of the shame, guilt, and insecurities that plagued me. Whether it was talking with a therapist or a good friend, I would eventually disconnect and dissociate from the truth, from the honest story of my life. Instead, I gave a more "cleaned-up" version, and I always presented well.

In mid-conversation, my mind would switch suddenly to something entirely different than the unvarnished truth, completely avoiding the opportunity for anyone to even remotely figure out my deepest, darkest secrets. I'd offer up the smoke-and-mirrors version instead. It was a self-defense mechanism, one driven by my younger years.

I was working with a writing coach once, trying to develop the thoughts I've now laid bare in this book. She, too, noticed my shame-based inability to tell the real truth. "You're telling a story, but I see no emotional connection between you and your words," I recall her telling me. "You're telling me these things like you simply read about your life somewhere and weren't even a part of it." She told me I needed to dig deeper, to connect with the soul of my story and tell it like it actually happened, emotions and all.

On these preceding pages, I've tried to do just that. To dive deeply, then resurface and write about my life in a way that will help my readers understand the power of their own stories and their own truths. Dive. Resurface. Write. Dive. Resurface. Write. Repeat as necessary.

The passing of time, admittedly, has helped me dive deeper. Pain tends to ease with time, while the lessons learned from that pain often remain vivid and unaltered. With time, I've grown into my wounds. The scars within me today are like the index pages of my life. I can touch a scar, and a story comes forth.

Sharing my story with the world in black ink is one of the most challenging endeavors I've ever undertaken. The discomfort of unveiling my inner self is akin to the pain of childbirth. Nevertheless, this remains my story and my song, uniquely mine.

I laid it bare.

In this sense, this book has been like exhuming a body that's been dressed up, placed in a casket, and buried six feet down, assuming that no one will ever see it again. The eulogy has been said, the mourners have eaten well, and the repass has been left. A hard rain has fallen on the gravesite, and in the springtime, grass covers the once-fresh dirt.

But then we dig it up, and in doing so, we are forced to deal with what we see before us—even if doing so is unpleasant, painful, and triggering.

To exhume a body is to admit there's something you forgot to do. Metaphorically, I exhumed the body because I'd forgotten to—I needed to—tell these stories as they really were and as they actually happened. This exhumation, or digging deep and reporting the facts with unadorned candor, was QUITE scary! But my life needed another examination. Grief taught me that. My stories, those memories, and the emotions that I'd buried alive 33 years ago **ALL** needed to be exhumed. My aspiration for doing this is to impart a legacy of words driven by a sense of purpose that transcends mere storytelling. This, I believe, *is* my profound calling.

After living spiritually dead most of my life, I needed to perform an autopsy on myself. It had to be done! This was a divine order given by God Himself when He met me in the pit. He heard my prayers and met me at rock bottom when I called on Him for help. If ever there was a real-life example of the Parable of the Lost Sheep (Luke 15), my life is an example of exactly that. And you, dear reader, are holding the forensic pathologist's report in your hands right now.

I don't mean to sound cliché, but God told me to write this book. The very day of my meeting with God, when I gave Him my yes, He made it very clear that I would write this book; He even gave me the title. It was very clear that it was His divine order and directive as part of my yes.

He first gave me the revelation long ago, when I was 19 years old, and I hadn't even begun to live half the life I would live at that point. I told a family member I was going to write a book about my life. I had never shared that with anyone, and I can't say I'd ever thought about it before. It was as if it was spoken through me.

Once I said it, those words, write a book, took root inside of me: When Sherman killed that innocent 22-year-old mother in front of her children.

When my baby girl Brittani suffered from cancer and passed away at the young age of 22.

Throughout all the years of abuse.

When I found myself pregnant at 15 years old.

When I put my miscarried baby in a Ziploc bag in my bedroom dresser, and later in the hospital alone, desperate, and afraid.

When the girls in the neighborhood were being mean and judging me.

When my big sister Jeannine passed away so tragically and suddenly.

When my family was couch-surfing as a way of life.

Even when I felt my life slipping away in the emergency room as my heart was being shocked back to normal rhythm, I now see it all as early prophecies.

Not that God caused any of it, but that He preserved me to *redeem* it. Every traumatic event didn't just happen to me—but *for* me, for a greater purpose. What once felt like pain without meaning now stands as a signpost: a moment marked with hidden treasures and divine insight.

God didn't appear to me as a burning bush or scratch an outline in stone tablets from which I'd prepare the manuscript, yet He revealed it to me through the desire that He placed deep inside of me to become a writer. I've got no doubt about that.

He said that He will use it all! The good, the bad, the ugly, and the worst parts of my life for His Glory.

When the Lord asks, we've got little choice but to comply. Because I can attest that your purpose *will* chase and pursue you. You cannot outrun or hide from it. It will keep you awake at night. You won't find rest, and neither will your spirit be settled, unless and until you are walking fully in your purpose.

He allowed the events in my life, the scars on my soul, knowing someday I'd put them down on paper (Rev 12:11), and yet *still* proceed to give Him all the glory for the salvation of my soul.

God literally pulled me from the brink of death and out of the ashes from which each of these pages has emanated. I'm still here and survived it all **ONLY** because of Jesus' sacrifice, God's mercy and favor, and Pastor Simon's obedience to pray and intercede on my behalf.

Because He has a distinct purpose for my life, I now know everything He brought me through was preparing me for that higher purpose. I am absolutely astounded that He calls me His daughter, Healer, and Intercessor. The worldly things I used to make up my identity, the many masks I wore, are worlds apart from the identity I now have through God.

Many years have passed since the beginning of my healing journey, and I've finally reached the full circle point of restoration. The seemingly wasted years are being restored (Joel 2:25-26).

In my lifetime, I've covered myself in many garments, mostly masks, trying to hide the shame and insecurity that accompanied it. I've sought out different locations in which to live. I've swapped significant others. I've tried to bury traumatic memories and horrific acts beneath layers of symbolic masks and clothing, trying desperately to conceal a flesh that is worn and real. I've covered up aspects of a life I've often felt ashamed of, only to experience other events that required me to cloak myself even more. I was literally a walking laundry bag.

I've tried to remain completely open and transparently naked while writing this book. Or better yet, I had to come completely out of the darkness to walk in the light of healing, wholeness, and freedom.

When God told me to write my story down, He also told me to strip down bare and get to work. "Take off those layers of masks that are covering up your beautiful naked soul, and tell your story to the world. Remaining hidden doesn't serve Me or you! How can anyone know just how far I brought you if you remain hidden?"

To transform your life, you've got to first be free. I've only ever known how to be a prisoner. As a prisoner, our days are controlled by others. Prisoners are told what to wear, what time to rise, and when to shower. Others decide our meals and our bedtimes. They read our mail and keep us in our cages.

Freedom is quite expensive, too. It doesn't come cheaply regarding relationships, social status, or even peace of mind. Escaping from prison is a hard thing to do. You might die achieving your freedom, but at least you will find yourself free.

As for me, I am more alive than I've ever been.

In 2020, I embarked on a mission trip with my church to Honduras—a novel experience for me. Our purpose was to spread the gospel, share Jesus' uplifting message, and endeavor to touch lives.

His transformative influence can truly alter one's course. I had the opportunity to communicate aspects of my personal journey to the inhabitants of this stunning yet profoundly underprivileged nation in Central America. While pain and hardship know no boundaries, so do hope and transformation.

On February 16, 2020, I was baptized in the Caribbean Sea in Tela, Honduras.

I walked into those beautiful sparkling waters seeking to complete my transition, submerged by my pastor in the name of the Father, the Son, and the Holy Spirit. I emerged as a publicly convicted and redeemed daughter of God. The transformation was complete, and my life has not been the same since that day.

As I said, healing is a journey, and I'm very much still healing. Trauma, of all forms, requires ongoing healing. I'll always be healing because I'll always be pursuing a higher understanding of this thing called life and my purpose in it. As I become more of my higher self and continuously refine in this healing space, I'm learning more and more about my identity in God.

No human being is ever fully complete, after all. We'll breathe our last breath and still be evolving, still changing, fundamentally or in barely noticeable increments. But I'm a better, more complete person today than yesterday. I hope that tomorrow, I will be an even better version of myself.

Perhaps, like you, I've always been a believer. I always knew God was somewhere close by, watching over and keeping me from falling into *any* abyss. There were times He felt farther away than He does now, but in retrospect, it was I who couldn't see or feel Him because I had moved away from Him. He was there, always right by my side and oftentimes carrying me even when I was unaware of it.

My baptism was a way of rededicating my life, first to Jesus, then to myself.

Since then, I've changed my last name to that of my dad, Richmond, whom I wrote about earlier in this book. In a divinely orchestrated moment, the legal name-change order was made final on my Dad's birthday. I made only cameo appearances with my dad's side of the family during my youth and young adulthood, but today, they're truly *my* family.

My dad's side of the family was always a traditional one in the classic sense—dinner together, shared celebrations, family time, and reunions. I envied that as a young girl, and now I cherish actually being part of the family. They've welcomed me with open arms and embraced me tightly after being absent for so long. This family integration has made the puzzle of my life complete in a sense as well.

Over time, I've made intentional steps to reunite with other family members, as well as my adult son and daughter, who are 22 and 26.

As I've mentioned, freedom doesn't come without effort and isn't achieved without cost. The cost of my divorce was seeing the relationships with my children wane. They were prisoners of our war—their dad and I. Yet our children are on their own paths of healing, and I'm leaving these breadcrumbs behind, hoping they'll eventually find their way back to me. With time, patience, and the grace of the Lord, I believe that our time apart will fade into the past, and our restoration will stand as a testament to God's miraculous work.

Today, I am free! I mean absolutely FREE!

Free from everything and everyone that broke me. Free from anything that intends to keep me down. Free from disabling anger. Free from self-doubt. Free from paralyzing insecurity. Free from the guilt and shame I assumed when Sherman committed the murder days before I gave birth. Free from self-hatred, self-affiliations, and self-sabotage.

I've had to bury a child.

I've had to bury living relationships.

I've learned that life is written in pencil, not pen, and you're always wise to have a big eraser nearby, just in case.

In my time on earth, I've learned I can't sit back idly and allow life to happen to me. I MUST HAPPEN TO IT! With God by my side, His word rooted in my heart and in my mouth (John 1:14), I can overcome anything in this life regardless of the circumstances that have shaped it, despite the hand I'd been dealt. Nobody gets the luxury of playing victim forever. Woe has an expiration date. I can produce the future I desire by coming into agreement with the word of God and continually speaking it over my life. Like in Jeremiah 29:11, "For I know the plans I have for you."

*My grandfather hadn't appeared since my early 20s after Brittani was born. He'd died many years ago. Grandpa showed up back then when I was deep into despair, when I was young and fearful of a life that lay ahead.*

*So much had happened since those early days. Some of it good, much of it bad. So many people had passed. So many things had changed in my life.*

*He stood there, looking at me, his hands in his pants pockets, his church keys tinkling away like the sound of baby angels, a slight grin on his face.*

*"How have you been?"*

*"Oh, Grandpa, it's been so hard. So very hard. My baby, Brittani, well, she—"*

*"I know, Tami," he said, cutting me off before I could finish.*

*"And then the man I married, well, he got into drugs really bad, and one night he—"*

*"I know."*

*"And then I got remarried and—"*

*"There's no need to tell me, Tami. I know the story. I felt your pain. I saw and felt all of it."*

*My grandfather stood in front of me, half-smiling, seeming to absorb me with his eyes.*

*"Do you remember the message I gave you, Tami? Do you recall what I said the last time we talked?"*

*"Oh, yes, Grandpa. I do. I remember every single word."*

*He stood there, looking at me. I could tell he expected me to recite it back to him like a quiz answer or Bible verse. So, I did what I thought he wanted me to do.*

*"Back then, you said, 'You have everything in you already to over-come anything coming your way.'"*

*Grandpa let out a loud and hearty laugh. He was proud, and that's all I ever wanted was to make him proud.*

*"You're exactly right, Tami. EXACTLY right. Oh, you've grown to be such an impressive, strong woman of God. It's been great to watch your progress. The pleasure of my earthly death has been getting to watch your life from this place."*

*"But it's been so hard sometimes, Grandpa. Sometimes, it's been so—"*

*He cut me off again. This time, he put a finger to his lips as if to say, "Shhh."*

*"Everything that came at you, Tami, you overcame. You overcame it all," he said.*

*I looked back at him. I looked into myself. An unusual feeling of accomplishment and satisfaction seemed to wash over me. Perhaps Grandpa was right all along. Perhaps his message from long ago was spot-on.*

*I guess I had indeed overcome everything that came at me.*

*"You overcame it all," Grandpa said.*

*He smiled and jiggled the keys. And then, like Brittani, he was gone again.*

CHAPTER 12

# HEALED

*"Not all storms come to disrupt your life. Some storms come to clear your path."*

—Paulo Coelho

When my grandfather met me in my dreams and gave me the message of overcoming anything coming my way, I realize now that he told me that because he knew then I'd get to where I am now. He knew that God had called me higher, and I would be an overcomer, not just overcome my own circumstances, but go forward, heal, and begin to assist with breaking the generational curses in our family.

In one of the chapters of this book, we talked about rock bottom. I've always thought of it as the worst place you could be, but as I mentioned, rock bottom is *very sacred ground*. I said my most fervent prayers and cried the most desperate tears there. It's a dark place, but those desperate tears and fervent prayers cultivated the ground, and before long, new growth happened.

That is one of the principles I use today to know that it was something I could truly build on. I *had* to get to rock bottom (the end of myself) to find the rock at the bottom. In that space that most would despise or fear, God became God in my life right there in my pit. The previous foundation I had built my life on had to crumble to pieces and be destroyed. He brought me back to even ground and allowed me to rebuild a firmer, solid, and stable foundation on Him.

My life's journey and everything He allowed me to go through paved the way for my calling and mission. This path led me to establish House of Hope and Healing, a company dedicated to aiding individuals in breaking free from the chains of their past and finding renewal, particularly those ensnared in the cycle of grief.

Through the challenges and hardships I've surmounted, I've gained a distinct perspective on grief and a message of liberation in the grieving process. This revelation, directly imparted by God during my journey toward emancipation from the shackles that confined me, holds a singular significance.

After dedicating nine years to intensive therapy for grief and trauma, a profound understanding washed over me: my daughter Brittani comprehended her purpose with astonishing clarity. She held a deep comprehension of God's will and design for her life, even in the face of her cancer diagnosis and battle.

Through dreams and even a chance encounter with a stranger, she grasped the message not to fear or worry, reassured of God's constant presence in her life. She recognized that her transition to Heaven would spark my spiritual awakening, leading to my liberation through our shared journey. Her unwavering trust in Him and His plan led her to unequivocally say "Yes!"

This revelation struck me like the weight of a thousand bricks during a therapy session, leaving me in contemplation for a long time. My therapist was also speechless at the incredible insight this encounter brought forth.

Brittani knew her assignment here on earth, most especially at the end. She knew her yes to God was for a higher purpose and that it would set me free. Embracing and acclimating to this truth demanded both reception and acceptance.

You see, I brought Brittani into this physical world through an earthly birth, yet she, in turn, birthed and ignited a profound spiritual depth within me that I never would've experienced without grieving her loss.

How do you sit with such a deep revelation? It took nearly a full year after this profound realization to process it and begin to uncover the right words to convey its significance, not only in my life but also in my journey.

These words surfaced within a reimagined version of a song that had been a constant throughout my upbringing: "Mary Did You Know?" this time performed by Maverick City Music featuring Chandler Moore, Lizzie Morgan, and the Mav City Gospel Choir.

Upon my initial encounter with this rendition, the song remained on repeat for months as I absorbed every prophetic verse and revelation it contained. Each lyrical piece illuminated the reasons behind the trials I've endured in this lifetime. It was truly a remarkable experience with God!

Even as I write this now, a year later, my emotions well up in a way that defies description. My goodness ... When I contemplate the concept of love, Brittani's presence remains my epitome and embodiment of unwavering, altruistic, and sacrificial love. It leaves me pondering why she deemed me deserving of such affection. But I realize it wasn't that she saw me deserving; her love and obedience to God superseded everything!

Moreover, I reflect on why God saw fit to rescue and redeem me (Matthew 18:12 AMP). I am overwhelmed by the scope of this salvation! That single contemplation is a sentiment I'll likely carry with me throughout my time on this earth.

As I embarked on the journey of grieving for my daughter, it swiftly became apparent that I had no alternative but to retrace my steps through my past, delving into the origins of my profound anguish to discover where and when I lost myself. Where and when did I lose my voice? While her passing marked the initiation of a profound grieving process, it also served as a gateway into the depths of my heart and soul. Through this, I confronted the unhealed wounds that I had been carrying my entire life.

Grief was a transformative force that shattered me completely. This process necessitated years of breaking down, refining, purifying, and processing, as well as moments of solitude, introspection, and replenishing.

Eventually, I relinquished more and more control, allowing God to infuse my heart with a healing that only He could orchestrate. Through His intervention, my soul was resuscitated, and I was revitalized.

This expedition was an arduous and sometimes extremely painful journey, yet an essential one that guided me back to the very moment when I had initially abandoned myself and embarked on a path of spiritual dormancy.

I grieved the losses I had never grieved; I cried the tears I had never cried. I comforted, loved, and accepted the little girl who felt lost, abandoned, and hidden, and simultaneously recovered her in the process. At the core lay the origin of my healing: mind, body, soul, and spirit. I am just loving that little girl now and holding space for her.

The precise moment of revelation remains etched in my memory. It unfolded within the walls of the church during a Sunday service. There, I grasped the extent of the journey I needed to undertake—to backtrack through my past and delve into the profound emotional depths to initiate the healing process.

As I voiced my inner thoughts to God, saying, "I sense myself on the brink of spiraling," His response was swift and resolute. Before I could complete the thought, His reassuring words echoed through my being, "Without a doubt, you understand that I'll be there to catch you!" Overwhelmed with emotion, I wept intensely and surrendered to His guidance.

CHAPTER 13

# PAY ATTENTION
# TO THE HARD PAUSES

*"Celebrate the moment you've come full circle."*

–Kym Klass

I thought this book was complete after chapter 12 was writ-ten. I'd even communicated on all my social media profiles that the book was finished and provided a publishing date.

Then I ran into delay after delay and brick wall after brick wall. I noticed something was stopping me from reaching the finish line. I wanted so desperately to be done, but somehow, I instinctively knew I had to pay attention to the hard pause holding me back.

These delays seemed so bizarre and unnecessary. Initially, I thought I was under spiritual attack, and the delays were attempting to stop this God-ordained work. I even called it a spiritual attack to everyone I spoke to and began experiencing the intense emotions that came with this thought. I was upset, disappointed, and maybe even angry at what I perceived this to be.

In wisdom, I decided to *be still,* and I began to pray. In my prayers, I asked for two things—clarity and a divine resource to help complete this work. Once I prayed, I recorded a video to serve as a status update of my book. I hadn't prepared anything to say; I just expressed what came to my heart. I believe the Holy Spirit spoke through me, as what came forth was a profound message: "Pay attention to the hard pauses in your life."

As I sat with this word over the past three months, it began to bear fruit within me. I learned, grew, and gleaned from it. Ultimately, these hard pauses taught me one incredible truth: this book was not finished at chapter 12. It was missing some hard truths I hadn't yet unpacked, which I began to live out the moment I realized I was experiencing a hard pause.

This season of my life has been one of the hardest I've ever experienced! That's saying a LOT, considering the story I've laid out in the previous chapters. The transition to this season began when I knew I had to leave my job with a company where I had worked for nearly 20 years.

If I'm honest, I knew my time was up. I'd maximized everything I could do there, and it was past my time to transition. I had felt the prompting to leave for many years, but I didn't heed it and instead grew more and more comfortable in my role. When it became apparent I had no choice but to sever ties, it was extremely painful! I went through months of grieving, which I know now was more refining.

During this refining period, the pain of this mask being suddenly ripped off caused me to dive deep into the emotions behind it. I sat with them long enough until they finally revealed their names: shame and fear.

Shame because the job served as a good cover-up for the fact that I never graduated from high school, which most people in my life don't know about me. The truth is, I am a high school dropout. I hid that fact behind the mask of a pretty nice career path and a matching resumé. I am well-spoken, smart, and resilient. The lack of a high school diploma never hindered me physically, yet it mentally haunted me for decades.

At a very young age, I set my eyes toward "making it" to defy the words once spoken to me when I was 19 years old and first became a single mom after leaving Sherman. "You are a high school dropout and a single mom? You will never be anything more than that. You'll have to rely on welfare, you'll have more babies, and that will be the extent of how far you'll go in this life."

This fueled me, and I did everything in my power to prove that person and those words wrong. I was EXTREMELY driven and climbed the corporate ladder through a lot of hard work, but it often came at the sacrifice of my time as a wife to my second husband and a mom to five kids now.

During this refining period, I realized I had to finally face the question, "Who am I really without the mask of this job?" I also had to face the truth that this was yet another mask I wore to hide my true identity. I served *it* more than I served God or my family.

This was another painful removal that felt like it was violently ripped off, but truthfully, I probably wouldn't have voluntarily removed it myself. As I continued to grow and evolve, it no longer fit or made sense for who I had become.

With this realization, my spirit felt incredibly crushed. But I sat with this pain while simultaneously undergoing another round of trauma therapy. I painfully processed every single emotion that this season came to teach me and emerged feeling freer.

Ultimately, it brought me back beyond the words spoken to me when I was 19. The deeper root was a promise I made to myself at the age of 10 when I vowed that as long as I had breath to breathe, I would never be without my own home, and I would never go hungry.

The driving force behind the moment I made this vow was fear-based, stemming from the first time I witnessed a truly unhomed person selling tires on the side of the road. Without explanation from an adult or any prompting, I simply decided that would never be my fate. This memory and realization brought forth an incredible breakthrough for me!

I soon began noticing familiar patterns—moments and experiences that felt eerily similar to ones I had lived through before, almost as if it were déjà vu. It's hard to explain, but it felt spiritual. From the smallest things, like seeing signs I hadn't come across in years, to the more significant—revisiting health issues I had already overcome—it was as if life was bringing certain things full circle, nudging me to pay attention.

This happened so often that I finally asked God why it was happening. The answer didn't come right away, but I began seeing the actual words *"full circle"* seemingly everywhere I turned. Again and again, those two words appeared—on signs, in conversations, in random places—almost like breadcrumbs leading me toward a deeper understanding.

So I asked more specifically, "God, what are You trying to tell me?"

Again, the answer didn't come immediately, but I kept asking. One night, I woke up around 3 a.m., which I often do, to use the restroom.

When I returned to bed, I heard the audible words, *"It's because I'm restoring your years."* MY GOD! What?! I cried and prayed and thanked God. What a powerful message of confirmation!

The next day, while journaling, I searched Google for the words "full circle." I came across an article by Kym Klass published in the *Montgomery Advertiser* titled "Celebrate the Moment You've Come Full Circle." My dad is from Montgomery, Alabama, so this especially stood out to me.

*The moment itself is full of promise, of a hope not previously seen on the horizon. It is a moment when, after months of struggle, you stand atop a hill and raise your arms in victory, knowing the commitment it took to get there.*

*The past few weeks have focused on letting go, acknowledging anger, and living in the moment. It has been a journey. Mine. Yours. A path taken because something hit so hard that you had no choice but to push yourself up off the ground. It is a reality in life that will not hit us just once but again and again.*

*It is a reality that provides us with the tools to survive, no matter how difficult or inconvenient to our daily lives. That's why it is so important to stand upon that hill and raise those arms. It matters because you battled depression and came out stronger than before.*

*It matters because you finally found the courage to stay. Or to walk away. It matters because you finally learned why decisions were made. It matters in lifting your arms because you finally understand where you stand in life, with yourself. It is a life returned to you—a life you have always deserved.*

*When you are given the tools to come full circle, you can appreciate where you've come from, where you are, and what you have to do to stay there.*

*So often in life, we go the full circle. Off we wander this way or that, even for years, but one way or another, we often find ourselves coming back where we started from or somewhere symbolically similar. There are both major and minor circles to walk and live—www.inspirationandchai.com.*

*Sometimes, coming full circle only takes place within a physical location. You come "full circle" when you return to your childhood home and raise your children in the town or city in which you were raised. A lot of that is based on circumstances, decisions, and goals. But coming "full circle" internally with emotions and also years of what we might consider "damage" takes digging in to expose ourselves, our vulnerabilities, and our wishes for where we see ourselves.*

*And when we get there—here—we can more freely live. So, yes, celebrate. Lift your arms. Smile, and even if nobody else knows the work it took to get there, you know. And when this clicks, you'll know. It won't be the end of a therapy session or when you finally open up to someone.*

*For me, it happened on an early Sunday morning run this past weekend. After months of rebuilding inside, I felt free. After weeks of acknowledging anger, letting go, and living in the moment, I ran up and over a hill that I previously used to test where my strength fell on that particular day. On Sunday, there was no hesitation.*

*At that moment in our lives when we have come full circle, all components of wellness are intact. Take it. We know something eventually will fall off. A friend and I ask each other often, "It's always something, isn't it?" Then we laugh. You get one problem resolved, and the next day, something else needs to be addressed. It's not always a "full circle" type of problem, but enough to throw off our small moment of perfect balance.*

*Promise yourself that when you come "full circle," you'll find your way through the days and weeks ahead with the strength you know you possess to face whatever knocks you down again. Remember and understand the time it takes to get there, and remember to lift your arms high.*

As I read this article, I felt extreme chills throughout my body. The eye-opening wisdom from the words and the answers it provided for my life were quite startling, to say the least!

The words jumped out and literally grabbed hold of me as if they had been written just for me. They were like breadcrumbs from the journey I'd already traveled, allowing me to easily retrace my steps while simultaneously serving as breadcrumbs for the journey still ahead.

This was absolutely an encounter, and I thought, *Could this be a roadmap or blueprint for what God said to me about restoring my years?* I pondered and processed every word for several months.

I saved the article and referred back to it often for clarity as more and more full-circle moments began to transpire. Four months after my encounter with this full-circle message, my absolute worst nightmare came with a late-night phone call from my son Brian.

"Brian, what's wrong?!" I could hear the panic and sadness in his voice.

"Mom, it's Christian! Something happened to Christian, and I can't get a hold of my dad."

I asked Brian to slow down and said, "What's wrong? WHAT DO YOU MEAN SOMETHING HAPPENED TO HIM?!"

"Mom, Christian is in the hospital on life support! His friends said they found him unresponsive in his apartment after he didn't answer calls for several hours."

"NOT AGAIN, GOD PLEASE! PLEASE DON'T TAKE MY SON! HE'S AN ANGEL, AND HE'S GOOD TO EVERYONE! MY PRECIOUS SON, PLEEEAAASSSEE GOD NOOOOOOOOOOO!"

*"A path taken because something hit so hard, you had no choice but to push yourself up off the ground. It is a reality in life that will not hit us just once. But again and again.*

*And it is a reality that provides us with the tools to survive, no matter how difficult or inconvenient to our daily lives. That's why it is so important to stand upon that hill and raise those arms. It matters because you battled depression and came out stronger than before."*

The words in the full circle article burned in my mind the next morning as I felt the reality of losing another child. The desperate tears I cried, the fervent prayers I prayed, once again pleading with God and screaming from the core of my soul, asking Him NOT to take another one. The emptiness I felt in the pit of my stomach, the cruelty of not being able to just fix it—those emotions all came rushing right back in and completely rocked my world!

A plane ride to be with my kids as their dad rushed to Chicago to decide to remove Christian from life support left me raw, numb, and unsure where to place this compounded grief.

"I've been here before," I said. "I know how to grieve. I've found peace, purpose, and a new life with Brit's passing. I support and encourage other Angel Moms on how to navigate the cycle of grief. I've even found joy in the journey. But I don't know what to do with a second round of this." I was lost and utterly broken all over again.

As I arrived in Phoenix and greeted my kids—Bri, Brian, and Tiki—through our tears, we talked about each of our accounts of the last time we saw Christian and what was special to each of us about him. We shared all the memories we could muster at that time.

Then, I had a sudden realization. I told Bri (my oldest now) that God knew the heartbreak we were going to be walking through, and in His Grace, He gave us her newborn son, Cameron, who was just shy of six weeks old at the time of Christian's passing.

I said, "Babies are a heritage and a gift from God. Cam told God yes, and agreed to the assignment of joining our family here on earth. God knew we would need the love of this precious gift right now, and we must thank Him even in the heartbreak of this moment."

*"When you are given the tools to come full circle, you can appreciate where you've come from, where you are, and what you have to do to stay there."*

Although I knew God had imparted great wisdom in me and I had healed a lot at this point, I also knew I could not do this alone. I knew I could not survive this on my own strength. I survived the loss of Brit only by relying on my faith in God, Pastor Simon's prayers that covered me when I was in the pit, the community, and the word of God.

That is the only way I'll survive a second round of intense grief, and it was pretty clear that my reliance on God had to increase like never before. I began asking friends and members of my church to be my accountability partners, not to let me be alone for too long, to speak back to me the words of life that will keep me going when I don't have the energy or desire in me to speak them for myself.

As I write this, it's coming up on the second-year anniversary of Christian's passing, and I'm still deeply processing my grief. I'm sure I will be for quite a while … I still struggle to find the words that can accurately describe the pain in my soul, and part of me has found comfort in dissociating—again.

There's no manual for this, and there's a lot that comes with this that I just don't know what to do with. Silent prayers in the form of tears are all I can muster right now.

*"Promise yourself that when you come 'full circle,' you'll find your way through the days and weeks ahead with the strength you know you possess to face whatever knocks you down again. Remember and understand the time it takes to get there, and remember to lift your arms high."*

Not sure how to restart my life again or where to go from here, I returned to the place I called home—Texas—after spending a few weeks in Arizona. A new level of deeper soul-searching began, and I wonder how low I can possibly go? Not that I was trying to, and I certainly wasn't in the space I was when I wanted to die after Brit's passing. I just didn't have room for all of this—being an angel mom of two and all.

If I had to describe it, I would say my soul was wandering. I suddenly knew my life would once again never be the same, and what had defined me before Christian's passing no longer defined me. The remnants of masks that remained after Brit passed away, and everything else suddenly had to go.

I began examining every area of my life, wondering what made sense anymore. I asked myself why I did this or that, bought this or that, or kept this or that. And I knew it was time for another exhumation.

I drove to Chicago for Christian's second memorial and a volleyball tournament hosted by the college where he served as head coach. It would be an honorary game between his current school and his former school, both of which he coached over his career. It was an emotional game for all who attended and a wonderful tribute to his life, displaying the incredible impact he made on a multitude of people. I was simply in awe.

While in Chicago, I spent time doing more healing work. Whatever was driving me had to be an incredible force because what I was about to say made no sense to me, yet I knew deep down that I had to finally face my past life. It's been 33 years, and I knew it was just time!

I began by driving to the apartment complex where Sherman and I lived. I recalled the night I learned he murdered that young mom. I can still visualize every single thing that happened that night. I could even hear his footsteps coming down the hallway.

I sat in the car in front of the complex, recording my memory of that fateful night through painful tears as I released it to God and declared my freedom from this traumatic time in my life.

I then drove to the building where the bank used to be when Sherman made me withdraw my entire savings at gunpoint. Again, I recorded my thoughts and visualized the security guard saying, "Have a nice day" as he opened the door to let us out. Once again, through tears and prayers, I released it to God.

Next, I drove to the place where I worked when Sherman kidnapped me at knifepoint. I recalled sitting in the front seat of the police car, hearing the officer say he didn't want me to be another statistic of a wife murdered by her husband.

I took it all in and realized how I hadn't really healed from everything that happened in Chicago when I lived there. I ran from it and did everything I could to bury it, not realizing it was buried alive.

*"Things that are buried alive don't die, they fester and manifest in other ways and other areas of our lives."*

Yet here was my old life still very much alive by the sheer torment and anguish I still carried from it.

I drove around my hometown for a while, talking to God about everything I'd just recalled and asking for His strength to let it all go. To no longer be bound to the painful truths of my life.

After a while, once I had regained my composure, I decided to visit and spend time with my brother, Tim, and his wife, Kim, at their new home.

As Kim and I talked and connected more, I shared with her that I no longer felt my footing in the life I'd created in Texas. I felt a strong urge to sell everything I own and travel full-time, telling my story, volunteering, and going wherever God led me. I laid out my plans for how it would work and the thoughts I had on where I would go, what I would do, etc.

I waited for Kim to respond with, "Wait, what?!" She surprised me and said, "I completely see that for you, and I think it's your time to step out in faith to make it happen. It sounds like you're about to go home and do a serious purge." She saw me! My God, she sees me.

And I did just that! I was so encouraged when I left Chicago that I stopped in Indianapolis to see my cousins and share the buried story within me. They'd never heard it before, and I wanted to be sure as many of my family members as possible heard it from me before it was published for the world to see.

So I shared my story and cried through it. We shared apologies for the times we judged and held contempt for each other. Before I left, we stood in a circle holding each other, praying, crying, and prophesying to break generational curses from our family. Thank You, Lord!

I was so charged leaving Indianapolis that I literally drove through the night back home to Texas. When I arrived home and looked at the map to see the path I drove to Illinois and back, I could hardly believe it, but I'd literally traveled in a complete full circle. I KNEW this was no mistake!

As I packed up my home to embark on this new journey of discovery and freedom, I had to first purge everything! While going through and packing up my life, I began to realize that I had held onto so many things, beginning with my first marriage and continuing through the second. There was no reason to keep any of those things.

Suddenly, the only things that held value for me were family pics and keepsakes. Everything else had to go! I was so focused and intentional about this purge that it only took me three months to complete. By then, my home was leased, everything I owned was given away, and the only items I had were my clothes, my car, and items in a small 5x10 storage unit.

I was free and un-homed in a way, forcefully choosing to face that fear head-on while simultaneously chasing against the wind to discover yet another, new emerging me.

*"And when this clicks, you'll know."*

When I hit the road, I traveled south from Texas to New Orleans. I spent a few days in New Orleans, which is near and dear to my heart because my grandpa was born there. I also felt a deep connection there.

Next, I headed east and discovered a town called Orange Beach, Alabama. My hotel room overlooked the Gulf Coast. I spent many days and nights just sitting on the balcony listening to the waves as they crashed against the coast.

While there, I had high tea at noon at a quaint little tea shop in a nearby Alabama town with Stacy, a new friend I met through a digital nomad group on Facebook.

We talked and shared our hopes, dreams, and passions for nearly four hours, and when it was over, we both knew our meeting was meant to be. We left that quaint tea shop and small town like old friends who'd just spent the afternoon reconnecting.

Once I left Orange Beach, I traveled east to Cape Coral, Florida, and spent nearly four weeks there. I found a local church to attend, met another angel mom, and shared our stories of child loss with each other. I found confirmation after confirmation that I was meant to be in that exact place at that exact moment in time.

After leaving Cape Coral, I headed north to DC to spend a few weeks discovering the area. I met and reconnected with Michele in Maryland, who was an old friend and more like a sister. We worked together nearly 30 years ago in Chicago.

I also had a chance to reconnect and spend time catching up with my cousin Billy and Aunt Ruth from my dad's side of the family in Virginia. Next, I traveled to New York City, where I discovered the Diamond District and Manhattan, met new friends, and had the opportunity to tell my story to four people.

The connections I made after sharing my story were both electric and amazing. For some reason, I felt completely alive in NYC! God most certainly met me there. I felt His presence so strongly the entire time I was there, and I realized I'd found my voice again. Leaving New York was bittersweet. It will always hold a special place in my heart.

Next, I took a charter bus to Niagara Falls and experienced another full-circle moment there. Mom had taken Tim and me there as kids, when I was around two years old, and I have never forgotten how the falls looked when they were lit up at night.

The memory of the lights and the falls has been etched in my mind ever since. I had to go back! My time spent at the falls was majestic and nothing short of amazing. I felt another connection there, and a missing piece to my puzzle fell back into place. Oh, how I needed this level of freedom!

As the holidays quickly approached, I made plans with my kids to travel back to Arizona to stay from Thanksgiving through the beginning of the year. I felt a strong urge to get there quickly for some reason, and I couldn't shake it. I just *knew* I had to be there.

A week before I was scheduled to travel, I received a call from my daughter Bri. She told me that her dad just shared with her that he had to go into the hospital for a biopsy. Bri shared all the details and said she would keep me posted.

Initially, the news didn't resonate with me. I was on my way to lunch with a friend to catch up and pray. But while we were at lunch and I was sharing what was new in my world, Bri's words suddenly hit me. My friend and I finished lunch and prayed together.

Afterward, I headed back to the hotel where I was staying to process what I had heard from Bri earlier. While processing, I prayed, "*God, what is this? What does this mean? What do You want/ need me to know?*"

Before the day was over, the answer to every single question I asked was provided down to an exact diagnosis. I was not only laid out in complete shock and disbelief, but in intense grief at what was revealed to me.

I said nothing to anyone. I cried and prayed all weekend, asking for God's Will to be done and for His mercy. I figured it was best to keep this to myself until the biopsy results were received.

A week later, the results revealed everything that had been revealed to me the week prior: Stage 4 pancreatic cancer! Once the diagnosis was revealed, I prayed and pleaded with God, not for myself but for our kids, who have experienced the loss of two siblings and now the potential loss of their dad. "God, that's half of our family! Please have mercy and heal him."

My ex-husband and I are cordial. The war between us died a couple of years back on Christmas Day. He, I, and our kids stood in front of his home and talked for hours. It was a talk of healing, love, and peace.

I later thanked God because that was the day I finally got free from the anguish of our brutal divorce. It was a wonderful Christmas gift, and ironically, it was also the last day we all saw and spent time with Christian. Two incredible gifts in one day. God meticulously tied everything together.

While I had been praying for my ex-husband, sharing words of encouragement with him and the word of the Lord to help him understand his authority over any sickness, the disease advanced rapidly like nothing I'd ever seen before.

One day, out of the blue, I received a random text from him, *"I just wanted to reach out and say thank you for praying for me. You know the journey, as we have been through this with Brit. Your reaching out speaks volumes about who you are and have become, and I am so thankful for you and just being the person you are to do this. Thank you so much. Words cannot express what it means to me. Please continue to reach out and pour into the kids. They will need it."*

This immediately brought tears to my eyes and a deep sense of restoration and comfort to my heart. When I shared this text with Tim as a testament, he simply replied, *"Honor her for all her hands have done"* (Proverbs 31:31).

I knew the years I'd sown in tears were worth this one moment, one I'd never thought I would experience in this lifetime. The remnants of any lingering feelings of heartbreak from our season of war disappeared as quickly as they had appeared. I didn't realize then that this was also his way of saying goodbye.

He passed away on December 15, 2023—the day before Brit's birthday, 10 days before Christmas, and exactly 58 days from being diagnosed. Suddenly, the reason I felt the intense urge to come back to Arizona before the holidays made sense. I *needed* to be here for our kids. The very next day after his passing, I made the decision to relocate back to Arizona and plant roots here again. It just made sense, and the feeling of peace followed.

*"Promise yourself that when you come 'full circle,' you'll find your way through the days and weeks ahead with the strength you know you possess to face whatever knocks you down again. Remember and understand the time it takes to get there, and remember to lift your arms high."*

CHAPTER 14

# THE TESTING OF MY FAITH

*"Your training for a life of faith requires many areas of
learning, including the trial of faith, the discipline of faith,
the patience of faith, and the courage of faith. Often you
will pass through many stages before you finally realize
the result of faith—namely, the victory of faith."*

−L. B. Cowman,
author of *Streams in the Desert*

After closing on my home, the new year met me with testing of my faith like I'd never experienced before. Full
circle rapidly brought me to every single place I'd seemingly
failed at previously. I watched my life come full circle like a
movie on the big screen.

I wish I could tell you that I knocked every single test out
of the park like a grand slam champion in the World Series.
No, it was quite the opposite. At first, I had no clue what was
happening. I just knew it seemed as if ALL HELL had suddenly
broken loose in every single area of my life.

First, I was irritated, then I was angry, which soon grew into being angry *and* bitter, and I found myself complaining to whoever would listen. It became a vicious cycle to the point where I was sick of hearing myself complain.

Then I realized something else must be happening. Unfortunately, I didn't pray like I needed to initially because I was caught up in the whirlwind that had become my life.

My therapist of 12 years, whom I was now seeing again for weekly sessions, said something that made me think very deeply about my situation. She said, "God must really want you bulletproof."

The revelation that followed hit me like a ton of bricks. My faith was being tested. As I prayed with this newfound revelation, I realized very quickly that I needed to shut down ALL complaining. This was the time to pray without ceasing!

When I became quiet around those who were used to hearing me complain, a couple of them suddenly dropped out of my life as if they had never been part of it.

This was quite sobering! I thanked God for closing the doors that I was too blind to see due to all the complaining I had been doing earlier. I believe this stripping was to remove every mask that remained.

I can attest that this was absolutely the year that made me. My faith had been tested previously when Christian passed away, but not like this. This was all of the grief of the past few decades of my life and more!

Coming full circle and being faced with all the hard and damaged relationships I'd left behind when God removed me from this place was an incredible mountain to climb.

The years I was away were filled with healing, where God meticulously taught me and downloaded so much wisdom and knowledge into me that by the time I returned, I was nearly overloaded with His word and a deeper knowledge of Him.

Now I felt as though I was suddenly thrust into a position to actually have to "use" every bit of what I'd learned about praying, fasting, surrendering, binding, and rebuking until I became fully reliant on Him.

The warfare was intense, and I felt very much like I'd entered into multiple full circle after full circle moments that increased and eventually brought me back to that rock-bottom place where I had the meeting with God and called out, "*Jesus, I need you to help me!*"

The desperate place where God met me, and I gave Him my yes. The place where He promised to restore my family, because He said my yes meant I'd have to leave my kids behind at some point.

He brought me back to that very place where I had *no choice* but to fight the same exact battle, this time on my knees in prayer, KNOWING the guarantee of victory was on my side. Believing what I know and not what I saw in front of me.

He didn't pull me out of it right away either. This extreme testing lasted for most of the year. He allowed me to sit in it because I *had* to learn how to fight spiritually.

I can see how every test strengthened me in ways I needed to be strengthened, bringing about a level of confidence I had never experienced before. As a matter of fact, I'm writing these last few paragraphs of this book, wondering if there's more to come.

Yet, I still find comfort in Grandpa's words: "You have everything within you to overcome anything coming against you."

Yes, the testing of my faith was the hardest year of my life! With this newfound strength, I finally found the courage to step into a deeper level of faith through inner healing and deliverance.

I'd studied deliverance for about four years when my sister-in-law Angie first told me I needed to learn how to war and sent me the book *Pigs in the Parlor* by Frank and Ida Mae Hammond.

I had learned and said some self-deliverance prayers on my own, but I'd never gone through full-blown deliverance with a pastor or deliverance counselor, yet I knew I *needed* this level of freedom. Indeed, it was time.

Deliverance is God's powerful yet gentle way of setting us free—spiritually, emotionally, and sometimes even physically— from anything that holds us captive. It's not always loud or dramatic; often, it's quiet, personal, and deeply healing. Whether it's fear, trauma, generational patterns, or spiritual oppression, deliverance is the process of God breaking chains and pulling us out of darkness into His light.

In Scripture, it's reflected in Jesus' ministry of casting out demons and healing the brokenhearted. But it's more than just rescue—it's restoration. Deliverance is when the lies of the enemy are exposed, the truth of who we are in Christ is revealed, and lasting freedom begins. It's not just about leaving bondage behind—it's about stepping boldly into the purpose and identity God always intended for us.

I've been attending weekly deliverance classes and worship services that include mass deliverance for several months now, and I can say with absolute assurance, I never knew freedom like I know it now.

I've found a beautiful community of people who, like me, are hungry for healing and truth. This is something I've searched for most of my life.

I know I declared my freedom several chapters ago—and that was true then—but I'm even freer now. Why? Because I finally had the courage to confront everything. Absolutely everything that had ever kept me bound, broken, or buried beneath the weight of my past.

I discovered the generational curses and self-induced curses that led to infirmities, rejection, self-hatred, and everything in between. My life became an open book with the deliverance counselors. They learned and now know more about me than anyone in a close relationship with me.

Deliverance for me was like revisiting and discussing my entire life as far back as my very earliest memories, like swallowing those coins, hiding from my dad the first time I recalled meeting him, or suddenly remembering how around the age of 3½ to 4 years old, I wouldn't fall asleep at night until I heard "Theme from Mahogany (*Do You Know Where You're Going to)*" on the radio. Even now, that song deeply connects with me. I had a sudden knowing of everything I ever questioned.

One of the biggest breakthroughs came when I finally let God into the places I had tried to fix on my own—the deeply buried pain, the shame I had masked with strength, and the lies I had unknowingly agreed with for years.

In His presence, I didn't have to pretend to be okay. I didn't have to hold it all together. I could fall apart and be rebuilt, piece by piece, by His truth and His love.

There were moments during worship where I wept without understanding why—until I realized that I wasn't just crying, I was releasing. Releasing pain. Releasing fear. Releasing the need to control the healing process. And with each release, I felt lighter, stronger, more whole.

Deliverance helped open my spiritual eyes and ears beyond what I could have ever known or learned on my own. The missing pieces to the puzzle of my life not only fit, but suddenly everything I'd ever experienced made sense.

I deeply sense and understand the anointing, and that is when my spiritual and natural worlds connected. I will continue with the work of deliverance, staying free and eventually helping others to obtain this level of freedom too.

Day by day, step by step, and moment by moment, I am creating the life I love. As I leaned into this journey, I began having visions of what it might look like if every one of my heart's desires suddenly came to fruition.

I even started seeing myself as the highest version of who I was created to be—the *ordained* version, born from my renewed identity in Christ. The very version my best friend, M.O., saw in me and spoke over my life years earlier.

God knew He couldn't possibly have shown me all I'd have to endure before getting to this place because I surely would have said to him, "No thanks! I'm happy here being complacent and hiding from all things in life."

But when I think about everything and how long this journey has been so far, there is absolutely no way I'm turning back now!

In this season, I noticed that the more I prayed, fasted, worshiped, and interceded for others, the more this modern-day story of Job—my story—began to take a subtle but undeniable turn upward.

Slowly but surely, the deepest desires of my heart are coming to pass—one by one—in the form of eternal gifts. After all the years of turmoil, pain, suffering, trauma, the unimaginable loss of my babies ... from those valleys and long seasons of sorrow, to that life-changing meeting with God—the very moment where this book began—and through Pastor Simon's obedience in speaking fervent prayers of healing and restoration over my life, I never could have fathomed the glory on the other end of it all.

Yet even in the depths of grief, after my sweet baby girl passed, I found myself saying something I hadn't heard anyone else say—I couldn't imagine that God would ask me to suffer this deeply unless something greater was coming on the other side.

I had no evidence. No sign. Just a quiet truth planted deep within my soul long before it ever showed up in reality, that I couldn't stop speaking out. And now, I'm beginning to see it unfold—just as He promised.

Now I see why I *had* to reach this point before releasing this book to the public. I understand why its publication was halted over a year ago—because, spiritually, I wasn't ready.

I *needed* to be fully emptied of everything that came from the world, in order to fully accept the new identity I found in Christ, and *live* in it.

Everything that happened this last year was sent to enrich me, strengthen me, and prepare me for the journey ahead. It was nothing short of a true beauty for ashes transformation. And *now* I stand—*Un-Masked, Un-Broken, Healed & Set Free.*

> *"I waited and waited and waited some more, patiently, knowing God would come through for me. Then, at last, he bent down and listened to my cry. He stooped down to lift me out of danger from the desolate pit I was in, out of the muddy mess I had fallen into. Now he's lifted me up into a firm, secure place and steadied me while I walk along his*

*ascending path. A new song for a new day rises up in me every time I think about how he breaks through for me! Ecstatic praise pours out of my mouth until everyone hears how God has set me free. Many will see his miracles; they'll stand in awe of God and fall in love with him! Blessing after blessing comes to those who love and trust the Lord. They will not fall away, for they refuse to listen to the lies of the proud" (Psalm 40:1-4, TPT).*

And this is where the new chapter of restoration begins.

# EPILOGUE

A s we conclude this journey, I offer you a collection of narratives seamlessly connected to my epilogue. Within these pages, you will find journal entries—marked by dates and poignant scriptures—that have inspired and carried me through this incredible journey of healing, restoration, and redemption. Most were written *before* I ever saw any of it come to pass.

My hope is that these words resonate and stir something within you, igniting inspiration, strength, and motivation for your own path of healing and unmasking. When you encounter moments of discouragement or feel broken, revisit these pages.

And **NEVER** forget: God has the power to unmask, heal, restore, redeem, and set *anyone* free. No one is ever too far gone for our Father to reach them (Psalm 139:9-24, The Passion Translation). All He asks for is your FULL SURRENDER and faith to believe victory is guaranteed.

> *"Now to Him who is able to do exceedingly, abundantly above all that we ask or think, according to the power that works in us, to Him be the glory in the church by Christ Jesus to all generations, forever and ever. Amen!"* (Ephesians 3:20-21, NKJV).

## My Journal Entries

### *February 4, 2018*

You'd be surprised how many things fall into place when you learn to follow your spirit and speak with your soul. You've got what it takes to accomplish whatever your heart so desires, but it will take *everything* you've got.

Even if you go for it and it doesn't work out, you still win. You still had the faith to face something that frightened you. That type of courage and determination WILL take you places.

Be thankful for what you are now, and keep fighting for what you want to be tomorrow. One day, you will be in the place you've always wanted to be. When you let go, something truly supernatural happens. That is when you give God room to work.

### *February 13, 2018*

Sooner than you think, everything you're struggling with now will be a thing of the past. You'll understand why you had to walk through hell, and instead of seeing only what it took from you, you'll see everything it gave to you.

You're coming out of this! You're going to get your fire back. You're going to rise, not decline. You're going to prevail. Know this … it's quite possible that you're being used for something greater than yourself. Stay in faith.

### *August 29, 2019*

The people God uses to encourage, uplift, and inspire others are often the ones who've gone through absolute hell!

Yet, the miracle you need can only happen in the risky place called faith. Have you asked yourself how much your brokenness costs you? How much more is your worth to you? Because it will cost you that much more and then some! Make sure this is *really* what you want and then proceed.

## March 22, 2020

### Recovery at ALL Costs

My situations in this life won't define who I'm gonna be at the end of this refining process! If I were to look at my situations and life from the inside out without the lens of Faith, I can't even begin to fathom where I'd be emotionally. I mean, EVERY ... SINGLE ... THING in my life is uncertain right now. Everything looks bleak, and I seriously have *no idea* how things will turn around in my favor, as the word says, yet God continuously confirms for me that it will.

All I know is that my faith has *NEVER* been this strong, and neither have I ever FULLY relied on God the way I do now. I have no choice but to continue in surrender, although my back is absolutely against the wall with the world fighting against everything I'm running toward!

While I'm in the throes of battling against what it looks like vs. continuing to trust and praise God in the storm, the Holy Spirit gently reminds me in John 14:1-4, *"Do not let your hearts be troubled. You believe in God; believe also in me. My Father's house has **many** rooms; if that were not so, would I have told you that I am going there to prepare a place for you? And if I go and prepare a place for you, I will come back and take you to be with me so that you also may be where I am. You know the way to the place where I am going."*

Recovery still awaits me! The LAST thing I can afford is to allow *this* new chapter to place any doubt or fear in my mind. Yet, I recognize this is spiritual warfare and it ain't NO JOKE!

Truthfully, life was much easier before I decided to surrender my life and pursue righteousness. When I think about the storm and the magnitude it's manifested in my life, I can't possibly fathom what the scale of the victory might look like on the other side of it.

I have been in the wilderness for what seems like a lifetime! Hell, it's *been* an entire lifetime really! My complete awakening took *most* of my life to come about. It took and is taking EVERYTHING WITHIN ME to continue the pursuit of total healing and emotional freedom. I have to remind myself that most people don't even make it *this* far, so believe me, I understand how blessed and covered I am to have made it such a long way on this journey. I declare that I will make it!

My Grandpa (Big Jack) is often on my mind these days. I know he's looking down on me, bursting with pride as he smiles from ear to ear. I can envision him just like that right now. When I was a little girl, I would've done *ANYTHING* for his praise and acceptance. It makes my heart skip a beat at the thought anyway.

I give my Father in Heaven every bit of the glory of this birthing process. I'm eternally grateful for the joy-filled times as well as times of suffering for what it produced in me. The dark days I've traveled through and overcome never took away my ability to love and be loved, but in fact, tendered my heart even more and simultaneously strengthened my resolve to battle, war, and win in Jesus' name. Amen!

*You'll only enjoy the fruit of endurance when you persevere.*

**Jeremiah 1:5:** *"Before I formed you in the womb I knew you, before you were born I set you apart; I appointed you as a prophet to the nations."*

**John 14:27:** *"Peace I leave with you; my peace I give you. I do not give to you as the world gives. Do not let your hearts be troubled and do not be afraid."*

*This is my story, this is my song. And now that this bird has sung the song of all that was deeply embedded in her, she is no longer caged. She is free, and she still sings, yet the song in her heart is of a different tune. It has been transformed into one of beauty, from a place of healing, the oil of anointing flows from within. I would venture to say, she'll be singing beautiful songs from here 'til eternity.*

# ACKNOWLEDGMENTS

I am deeply grateful to my parents, who have been my unwavering pillars of support throughout my life. Your love, guidance, and sacrifices have shaped me into the woman I am today.

Mom, I'm so thankful for the faith you instilled in me at a very young age. During those challenging moments when kids at school treated me unkindly and turned away, your comforting words remained with me: "Jesus is your friend." This truth has resonated throughout my life, providing a steadfast foundation to lean on. Thank you for the legacy of faith.

Dad, I honor you for the hard-working, honest man you were, who always led with absolute integrity! You taught me so much about quiet strength, that the cost of peace is never too expensive. Your silent yet profound resilience has consistently served as an inspiration to me.

To my precious children, Brittani and Christian, who now watch over us from Heaven, your love continues to guide me. As long as I live, you will live, and I will honor your memories always!

Brit, you undoubtedly answered the call! You knew your assignment and confidently fulfilled it. It took me a long time to understand and see it. I'm eternally grateful to you and the GiftOfTime we shared. After God, there is no greater love. I love you infinity x's infinity.

Christian, thank you for trusting me enough to share your heart with me. Our sacred conversations over the years will remain with me always. Because of what you last told me, this book is now a reality. You also knew your assignment. Thank you from the bottom of my heart.

Bri, my love, you now stand in the space as the oldest in proxy of your Brit and Christian. A role I know you weren't ready for, but one you stepped into wonderfully. Thank you for encouraging me through the hard moments when life threw us a multitude of curveballs. You inspire me in many ways! Watching you now as a wife and mom brings me great joy. You're a gifted writer. I pray you pick the pen back up when the time is right. I love the beautiful family you and Shawn have created.

Brian II, my son, the one of the bunch who speaks my language, who still gives me a run for my money from time to time. You, too, inspire me when you allow the gift to flow through you. As you mature, I see more and more glimpses of it. You haven't always had it easy, but once you connect the dots and discover the hidden treasure of it all, you will be unstoppable! A higher calling awaits you, and I cannot wait to see it manifest in your life.

Tiki, my youngest of the bunch, you have and continue to keep me on my toes. You came into our lives and brought so much love and joy at a time when we really needed it. We've traveled to many places in this world together and shared some great memories. Your gifts are still being cultivated and maturing. I pray you will continue to walk toward them. Our journey together has not always been easy, but I'm grateful for the greatest moments we've shared between us, most especially our combined baptisms in the Caribbean Sea of Honduras. God knows!

A heartfelt thank you to my best friend, M.O. Your unwavering belief in me became one of the greatest driving forces behind my journey to fulfill this God-given assignment. Your encouragement, love, and support were invaluable as I embraced my authentic self and stepped into the higher calling on my life. You saw me before I could see myself—my higher self—the version of me that now walks boldly in purpose. You introduced me to her when I was still hiding, and you wouldn't allow me to settle for anything less. Thank you for teaching me, showing me, and speaking life into me. For nurturing what had been buried deep inside and calling it forth with such grace and conviction. Thank you for having the courage to travel the world with me, fueled only by the visions I shared with you. I honor you. I thank you. And though we may not walk side by side today, my life will never be the same because you were a part of it.

In loving memory of my beloved grandmothers, Grammy Alice Jackson and Grandma Estell Franklin, who were both angel moms, just like me. You both share an incredibly special place in my heart. Your love and legacy continue to inspire me, and my heart beats in rhythm with yours.

Grandpa Lawrence Jackson Sr. and Grandpa Isaiah Franklin Sr., you taught me so much about respect and honor, and about valuing what is good. When I think of Philippians 4:8, I think of you both. You are my idea of what this verse looks like lived out in real life. You were strong heads of incredible families. My life is richly blessed as a result of that solid foundation. I honor you. Thank you.

This book is a testament to the power of love, resilience, healing, and transformation. May it serve as a beacon of hope and healing for all who turn its pages. My desire is to create a lasting legacy through words, and this is only the beginning.

With heartfelt gratitude and love to you all.

# ABOUT THE AUTHOR

Meet Tami Franklin, a modern-day pilgrim on a profound journey of healing, faith, and transformation. Through her writing, coaching, and ministry, Tami brings a voice of truth, tenderness, and spiritual insight to those navigating life's hardest valleys.

Her mission is to help others unmask, heal, and walk boldly in the freedom of their identity in Christ. Whether on the page, behind a microphone, or in the sacred stillness of a prayer, Tami's words flow with purpose—quiet but powerful, like a storm that brings life-giving rain.

At the age of 48, Tami embarked on a transformative quest that took her across the world, gathering a wealth of diverse experiences. Along the way, she shared words of vitality and inspiration with those she encountered and dedicated herself to serving wherever and whenever she could.

A mother of five, with two now in heaven, Tami is the grandmother of three precious grandsons and one granddaughter who affectionately refer to her as Nina (Hebrew meaning: God was gracious and has shown favor).

She wears many hats. She's a Messenger of Hope and Healing, Inspirationalist, Certified Transformational & Grief Coach, Inspirational Speaker, Missionary, the Founder of

G.O.T. Foundation, Inc., a 501(c)(3) nonprofit organization, and House of Hope & Healing, LLC. These platforms allow her to serve those on a journey toward healing, helping others to transform their lives.

Tami's passion lies in inspiring and ministering to broken souls. Despite facing the devastating and sudden loss of her son during the writing of this book, Tami discovered an even greater amount of courage to continue serving the grieving community with unshakable faith and compassion.

Tami's gift of edification, her prophetic voice, and her anointed vision have made her the driving force behind the inspiring speeches "*If It Hurts, It CAN Heal*" and "*Rock Bottom Is Very Sacred Ground.*" Through her Grief Ministry, she seeks to help others find joy and hidden treasures within their own journey. She is on a mission to shift the global conversation around grief with one unshakable principle: *Grief is holy ground.*

Tami's global travels aren't just about exploration; they're missions of compassion to feed, clothe, and minister to those in need. She shares her story of redemption, the Gospel of Jesus Christ, and the truth of His word.

Her journey in Christ began as she grieved the loss of her oldest daughter. It was through seeking healing after hitting emotional and spiritual rock bottom that she discovered her true calling.

A divine encounter with God in 2012 ignited her path to share her story, a journey of healing that gave birth to the author and speaker she is today. Her voice now symbolizes the quiet, personal storms she faced along the way and the rediscovery of a long-lost strength she once believed was gone.

Tami's life is a living testament to the truth that God's promises of redemption are real, and the promise of restoration is available to us all.